Dog is a Love from Hell

Jimmy Cvetic

Illustrated by Rick Bach

A Special First Edition of 100 books,

Signed & Numbered by the Author & Artist

31 of 100

Lascaux Editions

© 2017 by Jimmy Cvetic & Richard Earl Bach
All rights reserved.

ISBN: 978-0-9891922-4-8

Front cover art by Rick Bach,
type courtesy of Rob Larson

Back cover photo by Duane Reider

The author would like to thank Charlie Deitch and Bill O'Driscoll for their support at *Pittsburgh City Paper,* for first publishing "I Caught Christ", "Just Because", "Pinhead the Fireman", "Junko the Ditch Digger", "Just Say 'Okey-Dokey'", "Pure as a Monkey Hitting you with a Hammer", "You Almost Bite a Guy's Nose off", and "Swearing".

Lascaux Editions
Bob Ziller, Editor

Printed by
Color Perfect Printing
804 Penn Avenue
Pittsburgh, PA 15222

Acknowledgments

I'd like to thank Bob Ziller, Rick Bach, Duane Reider, Elizabeth Meyer, Renee Sroka, and Gloria Sztukowski for patiently putting this all together, along with the Day of the Dog celebration, at the Roberto Clemente Museum in Pittsburgh. Much thanks as well to John Wheatley and his crew at Color Perfect Printing.
And my deepest respect for the law enforcement community, and all the people of this beautiful world.

To Gloria

Dog is a Love from Hell

Table of Contents

I Caught Christ	15
Lying to a Priest Ain't Like Lying to God	18
Tiger Rose Wine & English Leather	22
Zosha Palooka	25
Just Because	27
Becoming a Man	30
Loneliness Wears Smiley Face Underpants	35
Donna	39
God Knows What I'm Thinking	44
If Jesus is Your Friend …	46
I Ain't Buying that Slushy for You …	48
It's Not the Enema, It's the Fear of the Enema	50
First Pride, Then the Fall	52
Just Me and the Boys Having Fun	54
Murder on Christmas Eve	58
Surveillance	60
Street Justice	62
Art of the Jockey Strap	65
Reason Behind Reason Not to Lift the Seat	68
Pinhead the Fireman	71
A Whore's Story	73
Never Go Fishing with a Lawyer	76
If You Need Glasses, All Black Men Sometimes …	78
Just Say "Okey-Dokey"	81
25 Reasons the Dog Quit Drinking	84
Head in a Bowling Bag	87
Wrong as a Shit Sandwich with Cold Gravy	90
Amonti is Told the Secret, but He Just Forgot	93
Pure as a Monkey Hitting You with a Hammer	96
Blame It On the Lights	99
You Almost Bite a Guy's Nose Off	102
Soft Zephyr in Your Pants	106
I Don't Think there's a Law that Says You Can't Shit In Someone's Tuba, but Maybe There Should Be	109

Identity Theft and the Vanity of Your Worth	111
Two Thieves	115
Basset Hound	118
Dog Years and Treats	124
Big Jack	126
Junko the Ditch Digger	129
Happy Little Lamb Nursery School	131
God's Gift	133
A Great Place to Pick Up Chicks …	135
Hospital Gown	138
Nobody Ever Whacks Off and Thinks of My Friends	141
Swearing	143
Condolences are Condolences	145
Belladonna on Prozac	146
Another God Poem	148
Dog is a Love from Hell	151

Illustrations by Rick Bach

Dog's Paw	1
Sit Down, I Said Sit	3
Dunces Wild	21
Jimmy's Big Wheels	29
Bucket of Trouble	34
Lucky Strike	43
Three Amigos	47
Lady of the Evening	75
Still Life with Death	114
Cookie Jar	119
Howard	123
Bad Dog	140
Box of Skulls	150

I Caught Christ

Defining moments and milestones,
that is the *Ode to Joy*
Ode to Joy ...
I was an altar boy at St. Lawrence O'Toole
and proud as a rooster in my cassock
and this was in the days of Latin Mass
nuns swishing rosary beads
and drunks singing loud and off-key
smell of cheap wine
smell of incense
and the long dry sermons of Priests
who would babble on and on about sins of the flesh and
I guess I was too young to understand any sins of the flesh
except having the woo for Mary Sweeney who was
cute as patent leather shoes
and I guess that wasn't really a sin
because all the boys had the woo for Mary Sweeney.
I remember as if it were yesterday,
some would call it fate or
some call it chance,
but sometimes the stars line up and
I was serving mass for Monsignor Campbell
who was older than the Bible
and his Mass was longer than
a slow rosary prayed by an old nun on
a hot summer day ...
Anyway, I was assigned to carry the paten
as Monsignor distributed the Eucharist to all sinners that
wanted the body of Christ on their fat tongues.
I actually loved holding the gold paten
under the fat chins
and watched them put their tongues out,
and I know I'm not supposed to think like this
but I always wanted to whack a couple of those transgressors
right in the throat with the gold paten as they were gaping like
baby robins wanting to be fed with holiness.
I knew most of them from the neighborhood

and I knew some of them beat their wives and kids
and I knew a couple were falling-down drunks
and a couple of them probably ate meat on Fridays
and were probably responsible for the nails in the hands and feet
of Christ.
The fakers
the frauds
shams
phonies
but it was always the same,
they'd walk up and kneel down
and wait for the consecrated bread to be placed on the tongue
of those without sin
holy and pure
and I'd think: right
right
right
sure
sure
sure …
and always the same,
Monsignor would place the Body of Christ …
But one time the stars did line up
and I already told you, call it fate or chance,
Monsignor accidentally hit some fat woman on her fat lip
and missed her fat tongue
and dropped the host.
And I felt like Willie Mays
I saw the white host falling almost in slow motion
and holding my ground
and bing-bang
I caught the Body of Christ.
It landed in the middle of my paten
and everything became more holy,
like a Gregorian chant inside my head.
My heart was pounding like the church organ
I caught Christ
I caught Christ
My God

My God
I fell to one knee
I caught Christ
and a tear fell from my eye and I looked up at the stained glass
window of Saint Michael
slaying a dragon
and I knew I was blessed
and as I stood up I saw the rear end of Mary Sweeney
and just knew everything would always be alright.

Lying to a Priest Ain't Like Lying to God

Father Tom was a jerk
but most of the women loved him because he could sing really
well and was going to be an actor in New York.
Instead he quit the acting
and became a priest and I'd bet he just pretended to love God.
Every Saturday we had to go to confession
and the line along the wall was really long.
All the sinners waiting for their turn
into the little booth to confess their sins.
You didn't know which priest would hear your sins
because they would come unannounced
and then slide their nameplate into the holder.
Nobody wanted to go to Father Tom's booth
because he'd announce your sins to everybody in the church
by always asking you really loud to repeat your sin
and then he'd say your sin back to you really loud,
"You had dirty thoughts.
What kind of dirty thoughts?"
Father Tom always seemed to trick you
once you were in line
and he'd switch confessionals with Father Paul.
Father Paul was more forgiving,
and didn't announce your sins to the whole church.
And I wouldn't say it then, but
I can say it now … Father Tom was somewhat of a prick.
Father Tom would stop
and count the sinners in line
making sure he made good eye contact.
I always felt like he would have been an embarrassing apostle for
Jesus and would have stoned the sinning women when
Jesus told the mob, "Let those without sin cast the first stone."
I always pictured Father Tom firing a rock
quicker than Sandy Koufax
and conking the broad right in the head.
He'd do something like that,
and probably sing a song real loud,

hoping he'd become a parable in the Bible.
I pictured Father Tom even winding up with the second rock
and getting ready to wallop Jesus.
Anyway, I did like when he'd get some little sweet honey like
Mary Sweeney and tell the whole church her sins.
"You looked at what boys?
Looked at their behinds?
How many times did you look at the boy's behinds?
What kind of boys?
They were lifeguards at the swimming pools?
Did you look at the lifeguards anywhere else?
You looked at the lifeguards above the what?
Above the knee?
How many times?
You French kissed your boyfriend?
What do you mean French kissed?
You stuck your tongue in your boyfriend's mouth?
How many times?"
Mary Sweeney came running out of the confessional
all red face and blue-eyed crying,
and her face really stuck out because she had red hair
and lots of freckles.
Me and my buddies would be giggling.
Now, I know that you ain't supposed to lie to a priest
because you'll go straight to hell,
but if I had to confess to Father Tom
I'd always downplay my sins.
In fact, on purpose I'd leave out certain sins like
playing with myself
and unfastening bras or
where I might happen to get lucky and stick my finger.
I'd just go into the confessional and lie.
I'd always say things
like I hit my brother five times
stole cigarettes
and lied to my mother
and even lied to my friends.
I'd always say ten times I lied
but then change the number of lies to eleven,

"Better make that eleven, Father."
Because I knew the bold face I was lying to Father Tom,
and I also figured God knew I was lying,
but God wouldn't want Father Tom to conk me with a rock.
After I was done with my lying confession,
I'd make sure I'd kneel right behind Mary Sweeney
and I'd look at her cute little bottom.
I'd whisper,
"Mary, I'm planning to be a lifeguard next year."
She'd giggle
and I'd giggle right through my nose.
Then I'd whisper,
"I'm looking at your bum,"
which made her face turn redder.
"You just came from confession, you little pig."
I'd go, "Oink-oink," and giggle
again right through my nose.
Me and Mary would leave church,
sneak down the alley
and we'd hold hands and kiss like we were in France
and prepare for next week's forgiveness.

Tiger Rose Wine & English Leather

Some people are not meant to be thieves,
nor should they ever take the vocation of a driver
for bank robbers,
nor should they ever take up the profession of
safe crackers or forgers,
or pickpockets, and
I learned this early in my life,
having been caught too many times in the cookie jar
with my pants down.
I was just sixteen with a ducktail attitude
hormone happening pimples and
swagger of a wannabe pimp
or rebel with a cause wearing tight blue jeans
English Leather smell like sin and
a swagger to make mothers lock their doors
pray novenas and hide their daughters, but
so were most of my ugly friends, not much better and
just wild side ignorant boys growing up with growing pains in
Pittsburgh.
I remember playing forty-seven days hooky
from school and
we'd go skinny dipping in the river
under the bridge in the Allegheny
bare ass bold we'd pee like the gods gave
us the ability to hose down Northside in urine.
When we were done swimming and peeing,
Howie, who just got out of Thorn Hill, said,
"Let's rob the pretzel man."
Me and Mouse said,
"Yeah, let's rob the pretzel man."
We walked with our wet jeans stuck to our ass
and while Mouse distracted the pretzel man
me and Howie snatched a handful of the warm pretzels
and ran our skinny to the bus station and stuffed our bellies
with the feel good warmth.
Then Howie said, "Let's go to Kaufman's and

steal some cologne."
I said, "Let's steal some alpaca sweaters
and we can snitch the cologne up the baggy sleeves."
Mouse said, "Great idea."
So we made our way to Kaufman's and
stole sweaters and enough cologne
to make an unflushed locker room smell good.
Then Howie said, "Let's steal some cigarettes."
I said, "Sounds like a plan.
Let's go to G.C.Murphy's and we can stock up on
some cologne and good French cigarettes."
Mouse said, "I'll watch the door."
Howie said, "I'll watch for the cops."
I said, "I'll get the smokes."
As my hand cupped the cigarettes
a big hand grabbed me by my collar and
dragged me back to a little room
followed by Howie and Mouse, and punched me in the belly
and slammed me into a wall hard enough to knock a couple of
pimples from my puss.
After slamming and choking
I was forced to sign a confession
and a call was made to our mothers proclaiming us thieves and
the pricks even called the school and we were caught bare ass.
I was brought in front of Mr. Edget who was going to boot me
out of school right into the Marines,
but my dear sweet mother's tears
and three quick swats across my opportunity
saved me from an early boot camp.
I was on probation forever and forced to punch a time clock
at school and grounded
and was told, "You stay away from those bums,
that hoodlum Howie and Mouse are going to send you
straight to hell on roller skates."
I said, "Yes, m'am."
And I was grounded for two weeks, scrubbing walls
and washing windows
scrubbing floors
and dragged to church till I convinced my mother

my halo was shiny again and had less of a tilt.
I asked my mother, "Can I go to the dance tonight?"
She said, "Alright, but you stay away from those thugs."
I said, "Yes, m'am … and can I borrow two dollars?
One to get into the dance, and one dollar
to buy a girl a Coca-Cola."
She handed me the two dollars
and I was off like I was wearing roller skates.
I hooked up with Mouse
and we went right to the State Store and bought
two quarts of Tiger Rose Wine.
We hadn't walked a block when Officer Haggy
jumped out red lights flashing and
snatched us into the back of the wagon like we
were blessed with amazing grace.
Don't think I was gone more than fifteen minutes
when Haggy had me standing tall by the seat of my pants
in front of my mother, showing her the quart of Tiger Rose
and she hit me with a quick left hook
that could drop a water buffalo,
"A dollar for a girl and a Coca-Cola."
I picked myself up from the floor and was grounded forever,
and Mouse and Howie disappeared like an old song
and cheap cologne,
rot gut wine, and
in a sad way, Vietnam claimed us all.

Zosha Palooka

I remember and still almost feel the pain
of my first love
a healthy Polish girl
with thick legs that carried a round rump
which till this day reminds me of a small pony
hauling and pulling around a small fruit wagon
and to tell you the truth I almost
gave my heart into forever and
I almost got a heart tattooed on my bicep
with her name Zosha Palooka on a pair of boxing gloves
but I'm really glad that I didn't because
little did I know that in spite of all the pierogis
that we shared that she would one day break my heart.
I sometimes less than often think of Zosha
and how I went off to war pretending to be a hero
and absence does not make the heart fonder
any more than a wet dream
and I'd write her love letters
from the trenches of the heart
and tell her about battles that I never fought
except maybe in my mind when I was carelessly tossing around
truth like I was walking a tight rope juggling plates
or maybe wrestling alligators
or running into a burning grade school to save innocent little girls
or maybe the United States Constitution or
maybe even catch the falling flag with my wounded outstretched
arm before the stars and stripes fell to the earth in the smoke
of battle
but always only assuring her that I was just doing my job
and what was expected
of any red
white
and blue
apple pie eating boy from Pittsburgh in the defense
of our steel mills once owned by Carnegie
and the Hungarian work ethic of all those long underwear men

before me that ever laced
on a pair of steel toes who also loved deeply and
hunkered their way to work
who just knew love like the warmth of a radiator
and morning mouth of root soup.
And as sure as love owns desire,
I loved her enough to fill a bushel basket with puppies,
but anyone that ever loved knows that puppies will keep you
awake at night
even if you let them sleep with a warm water bottle and an alarm
clock.
But all young love fades like a spinning bottle
and a pinched nipple
except maybe the memory of a sore toe stepped on by
a soft-bottomed girl named Zosha Palooka
and in my memory
spinning
spinning
spinning a Pittsburgh Polka
I loved that kind of love
of almost a tattoo
and a small pony pulling a fruit wagon.
But as war hardens all hearts
I truly hope she is almost always happy and
weighs no less than three hundred and fifty pounds
and sometimes gets kicked out of Weight Watchers for
wolfing down just too many salami sandwiches but
with her thick legs and chubby feet she still can stomp out
just one more hoopi-shoopi polka.

Just Because

I know there are things that you ain't supposed to
do and will probably get you a good whipping
if you're caught but you'll do them anyway
just because and for no other reason than just because.
Like you ain't supposed to play with matches
just because you can burn someone's porch down
or shoot marbles with a slingshot at a dog
just because you ain't
and you ain't supposed to tie two cats' tails together
and toss them over a clothesline
and you ain't supposed to fart in church
and you ain't supposed to rob the poor box
ain't supposed to stick anyone in the eye with an umbrella
and you ain't supposed to make pipe bombs
'cause you might get your fingers blown off
and you ain't supposed to stick bubblegum in anyone's hair
or put crazy glue on toilet seats
or flush cherry bombs down the toilet
and you ain't supposed to tell lies
but if you do have to tell a lie
do it bold face and make sure it's a damn good one
and if you get caught red-handed tell another one
and make sure your head is hung down
and mumble like you're really sorry even when you ain't
and you ain't supposed to swear unless you like eating soap
and you ain't supposed to hit your mother because
when you die your hand
will come out of the grave and a dog will pee on it
and you ain't supposed to tell your sister to swallow
a whole fizzy like it's a Communion wafer
because if she does her belly will swell up like she's going to have
a baby and rumble like Mt. Vesuvius and purple stuff will come
out of her nose
because she'll run crying blaming you for sure
and even if you hide in a tree your mom
will find you and you'll catch the switch

but it is something else to watch your mom climb a tree
with a stick in her mouth when she's mad
and you ain't supposed to go swimming butt ass in the river
because you might drown and be eaten by the fish
and you ain't supposed to throw anyone's tennies in the toilet
and you ain't supposed to play hook from school
and go downtown to shoplift
and you ain't supposed to steal cars
or catch rats and put them in anyone's locker
and you ain't supposed to sass or mimic
or put your palm up on a bus
and have a pretty girl sit on your hand because
she will sure enough get mad and think you goosed her
and she'll kick you in the shin
and tattle and nothing good will come out of it when
someone tattles on you for a goosing
and you ain't supposed to trick people out of things
like their bag of potato chips or their apple
because you'll have to pretend that you like them
even when you don't
and they will for sure want to hang around with you all day
and you'll have to douse them with skunk perfume
and sure as gosh-awful will be found out
because of a little crybaby telling
and you ain't ever supposed to find fun in kicking a pigeon
if you're caught you'll get the blame for stuff you didn't do
even if you blame your brother.
Anyway, I know boys
that never part their hair
or wash their hands
that lie and swear
and smell like the alley
and do fun things like this and that
but they weren't really bad boys
maybe just a little mischievous
but they weren't bad
and to tell you the truth I think some of these things
defined a boy as a man
and sure as all sin follows forgiveness

you ain't ever to look at a girl's behind when in church
because you could go blind and
because some things you just ain't supposed to do just because
but you do them anyway just because
and there's no other explanation, other than just because
and there's a good possibility you could one day grow up
and become the President.

Becoming a Man

I was reading Celine's book
Journey to the End of the Night.
And I fell asleep, the book heavy on my chest.
I woke half asleep at dark in the morning
and was back forty years ago in Bien Hoa.
I remember working the tower and looking over the fence line
through my binoculars.
I was in the tower for over too many hours
alone with too much time
silence and prayer
and thought
and masturbation.
Nobody will tell you, but when you're alone
with silence,
you pray
and sometimes play with yourself.
It wasn't entirely my fault
because I would look beyond the barbed wire
at the Buddhist temple
and see the bald-headed Monks with long white and gold robes.
They always walked slowly with their heads down
always
always with their heads down
into a white temple
and
I think they would go inside and pray.
At least, that's what I believed the Monks did when
they went into the temple
but sometimes someone on Buddha Hill would
shoot at us.
I can still remember the sound of a whiz of a bullet
and the crack of a rifle.
I was glad that whoever was shooting was a bad aim
or maybe I wouldn't be writing this poem,
but who knows.
Anyway, it wasn't all that bad sitting for hours in the towers

all alone because there was silence
except for the F-100's
and the Cobras.
That sound of the roar goes away
except inside your head you will always hear the roar.
Anyway, I'd sneak dirty magazines with me
and hide them under the sandbags.
Me and my relief knew where the magazines
were hidden and we never told anybody because
if the brass found out, they would surely Court Martial you
and send you away for dereliction of duty.
They would probably accuse you of thumping yourself
but only a fool would admit to self-pounding.
Now, as I said, it wasn't all my fault,
the young girl in the rice paddy surely
must share some of the blame.
Every day she'd come out into the field and work
and there was always a water buffalo
and hot sun.
It seemed like there was endless green water
all the way up to the Buddha Hill and white temple.
Almost like a postcard
except for the barbed wire, it was picture perfect.
I would watch the girl for hours,
she had such beauty and grace.
She had long silk black hair
that hung down her back
touching the top of her ass cheeks.
She would bend over all day,
hours led to hours picking rice.
I watched her.
Sometimes during the day
she would pull down her black silk pants
and pee right into the green water.
It was beautiful,
and she was beautiful.
I'd watch through the binoculars
and thought … she is not my enemy,
she's too everything and

if given a chance I could fall in love with her.
I'd even take her home with me
when this stupid war was over and I'd bet she'd love America.
I'd watch 'til my eyes grew tired
and continued to watch her pulling the rice under the all-day sun,
she was beautiful.
Sometimes, she would take all of her clothes off
and she would wash herself in the green water.
She would pull her white blouse over her head
long skinny arms
and she was golden.
Small breasts
skinny
long silk black hair.
Then she would pull off her black pants
and hang them on the back of the water buffalo.
I'd watch as she raised her long thin arms
and wash her pits
and then she would wash her small breasts.
She had skinny legs
and a small patch of hair
she was so beautiful and earthy.
I was so young
and even in war you can find love.
Young boys in war think of girls
and home,
as they say, apple pie.
One day the Colonel
came riding up in his jeep.
Everybody knew him because of his eagles
and his white hair.
I was afraid of him
and didn't really like him.
Ten months earlier, he had put me in jail
because I drank too much Vietnamese beer.
He let me sleep it sober
but he threatened to keep me in jail
if he ever caught me drunk again
and he made me clean the shit house

and fill sandbags
but he didn't take my one stripe
and I guess he could have if he wanted
but he probably felt sorry for me
because I had pimples
but I'm not really sure why and
never will because it's not like he'd ever tell me
and it's not like he'd even remember letting me keep
My
    One
        Stripe.
Anyway, I slid down the sixty-foot tower
when he pulled up with his jeep.
I cracked my best salute
because I knew Colonels like to be saluted.
But to tell you the truth
I thought it was a crock of shit
but I saluted anyway.
I don't remember much about our conversation
except I didn't want him climbing up the tower.
I figured he'd look around
and find the dirty magazines
and of course there would be an inquiry.
We made small talk
and I remember he remembered putting me in jail.
I asked him just one question
and I remember it even after forty years.
I asked, "Colonel, can I ask you a question?"
He said, "Yes, what is your question?"
I asked, "Am I a man yet?"
He winked and saluted as he drove away,
smiled, and shook his head.
I returned the salute
and climbed back up the tower all proud
picked up my binoculars
I felt the weight on my chest of Celine's book
and looked for the beautiful woman.

Loneliness Wears Smiley Face Underpants

All the guys liked working the whore details
but few would take off all their clothes
and expose their everything
I wasn't afraid of anything, not even my shortcomings.
We got a complaint from a swank hotel
that there was a whore infestation
and they needed a tablespoon of our integrity.
It was a hot August night
and the Lieutenant volunteered the squad
Me
Sco
Mikey Mike
Ikey Ike
Toddy Todd
Z-Girl
Big Head Murph
Strit
Joe So
Little Prick
and Shit Stirrer.
In fact, the Lt. sent me home to get my nerd clothes
sport jacket and bow tie
argyle socks and wing tips.
I even put on a pair of my
yellow silk smiley face underpants
and I must say
I was looking better than Fido's ass.
I go back and the Lt.
wires me with a secret microphone
which may have been in my belt
or shoes
or even my bow tie
but I ain't telling where the secret mic was hidden
just in case he ever asks me again.
Anyway, we test the secret microphone
one two

one two
testing
testing testing
and just like the Beatles
one two three four
It's been a hard day's night
and I been working like a dog.
Lt. said,
"Okay, I can read you loud and clear."
He then counted out
One thousand dollars of marked crisp Benjamins,
"Dog, don't front the money –
and remember to think with your big head."
I grabbed a handful of my personality and
Saluted, "Scout's Honor."
He said, "Okay men, let's saddle up."
Thinking back now,
he always said things like,
"Okay men, saddle up."
"I'd rather be judged by twelve men than carried by six."
"Get out of town."
"That's a mean-spirited horse, but like most men …
horses can be broken."
"We ride with the brand."
I thought he watches too many westerns.
He then told me,
"Me and all the guys will be in the connecting room
listening on the microphone
and when you say,
'High-Ho Silver' we come through the door like a stampede."
I knew why the guys would bust
in the connecting door
is mostly because they got to see the whore in the skinny,
a free ass and titty show.
Anyway, I go down to the bar and
sure as there's a price tag to love, I met Leona.
She's Spanish or Italian looking
fine black velvet
hot red luscious

sin smell good
all round and squeeze.
I buy her a tall glass of
feel good and
she drops off her six inch spike
and with her toes starts to rub and pinch my leg
and leans closer and with red hot wet lips whispers,
"Want to help a poor girl cure a lonely heartache?"
I asked, "How much does a poor girl need for the cure?"
She said, "Just a little bit,
Five hundred for a half hour
and on special tonight two hundred for each additional hour
of pleasure."
I showed her my room key,
and paid for the drinks showing her the Benjamins,
"Two and a half hours should cure the lonelyssssss …
let's not wasssssste a moment."
She put her hand around my stiffy
and we got on the elevator
and she bit my ear lobe
and grabbed my everything,
I said, "Let's move ssssssssslowly baby,
broken heart repair
sssssshould take more time than a handssssshake."
We go to the room and
she's on me like a snake whispering temptation.
I kind of stop her,
gave her half the marked bills
unbutton her blouse with my teeth
stuffing a rolled up bill into her bra
and she dropped her skirt
and she was red silk panties and soft mound
and I stuffed a couple of bills where they belonged.
She then pushed me down on the bed
and pulled one shoe off at a time
and then unbuckled my pants
and pulled them down
and that's when she
saw my yellow silk smiley face underpants and she

said right outloud into the mic,
"Aha! They're so cute!"
I said, "Say underpants, say underpants."
I'll just end the adventure here with "High-Ho Silver"
and the rest was told in the court of law.
Oh yeah,
Mikey Mike and Ikey Ike
and Z-Girl
and Sco
Joe So
and Strit
Big Head
and Little Prick
and Shit Stirrer came through the door just like a stampede
and got a free peep show.
And me and Leona never quite found a cure for loneliness.

Donna

I guess the first forty-eight hours are important,
at least that's what I've been told.
I remember going to the funeral home on a Saturday
and me and Brother Gru were taking license plate numbers
and just looking at the faces of the mourners.
We could sense something was wrong,
call it a kid caught with his hand in the cookie jar,
just too many hands and not enough cookies for everybody.
That's when we met Jack Knife Jimmy Lee who was sucking
on a cigarette.
He was from the Texas Mafia.
He was the first break in the shooting,
how he drove from Texas
all because he needed pain pills in Pittsburgh.
Second break was when we saw
Donna beat on Jack Knife Jimmy Lee.
We watched as she with a mean look was
pushing and finger poking him in his chest.
Me and Brother Gru watched as she pounded him,
"Something's wrong," I said, "why is she breathing thunder
and pounding on Jimmy Lee?"
Brother Gru said, "Let me find out
as soon as he comes out to suck on another cigarette."
Sure as a nicotine fit Jack Knife came back out
and Brother Gru finds out all kind of good stuff …
Like how he got his nickname Jack Knife because on a dark night
hauling a bed of black iron to Houston
just outside Detroit he hit some black ice and cut his eighteen-
wheeler in two.
Actually, he said, "I was coming down a goat hill
jackknifed three times
and slid sideways more than a quarter mile.
That's when the other truckers hung the handle Jack Knife
and it stuck like shit on a wall."
Just like a runaway eighteen-wheeler some things can't be stopped
and some men just can't help telling their versions of truth,

and it was just like hot water through a rooster
strutting in the barnyard,
shit drops everywhere.
Then the usual,
find and follow the money.
And sure as a high insurance policy
you can sometimes find a motive.
Now I want you to know the name Donna means Lady
and has roots in Italy,
actually means Lady of the Home.
Alright, Donna
was a pudgy dirty blond.
Too short and stuffed too tight skirt
high maintenance nightmare
lots of makeup and thick red lipstick
cheap smell good
and facials
matching fingernails
high heels clicking so you could hear her coming
just a fast red car woman.
But mostly a fake smile of a woman that sits at the end of the bar
at closing time holding onto two o'clock ticking
with forever hopes to find the slow dance of forever but
forever never quite arrives and
only the taste of whiskey promises and could have been
and a touch of silk sheets and fresh morning coffee.
But forever just is not forever for some
no matter how the clock ticks
and keep in mind the name Donna doesn't always mean lady.
Donna was the kind of woman that has an overstuffed drawer of
silk panties
and never enough shoes
never enough thick lipstick
or enough fingernail polish and
never enough maxed out charge cards and
good just is never quite good enough.
She was really that kind of woman.
Except Donna was a mean-spirited woman that
more than once caught her tit in the wringer.

And maybe just maybe that was why she was mean.
Tit caught just too many times in the wringer but
who can say what causes mean?
After all ...
she was the grieving wife
who could cry on cue without tears
and tremble just like a little bird on a cold January day.
She was real good at fake sorrow
but much better at calling up the insurance company and
demanding what was really hers.
Well, sometimes there are blood drippings on inheritances
and sometimes things just aren't right
and if things aren't right then maybe they're probably wrong.
Anyway, Donna met with me and Brother Gru
enough times to tell her story of sorrow.
She even tried to make us understand
why Jack Knife Jimmy Lee would come to Pittsburgh for drugs.
Well, one fib leads to another fib
and another and
then the first fib isn't just right
and the second fib is worse
and third
fourth and tenth is worse yet
and sure enough someone is standing in front of you
pants on fire with a nose as long as a telephone pole.
Every day Donna would ask,
"Brother Gru, did you find anything out?"
Brother Gru would say, "I'm working on it and
you'll be the first to know."
Always the same question, "Any news?"
Always the same answer, "I'm getting warmer."
Days turned to weeks
facts turned into malice and intent
and premeditation.
It's like you keep putting a feather on a mule's back,
enough feathers the mule falls to his knees and
you find out the weight of feathers.
Brother Gru went to meet with Donna
and she asked,

"Did you find out anything yet?"
Brother Gru said, "I have some good news and bad news."
Donna asked, "What's the good news?"
Brother Gru said, "We know who killed your husband."
She said, "Thank God."
Brother Gru said, "Let's keep God out of this."
She asked, "And the bad news?"
Brother Gru reached in his jacket and
pulled out a warrant,
"The bad news — it's you."
I guess the name Donna still means Lady
but instead of Lady at Home
it means Lady in Jail serving time without makeup
with no parole.
And Jack Knife Jimmy Lee,
he's serving forever without his truck
because you just ain't allowed to kill people.

God Knows What I'm Thinking

"You know, God, it's strange
that we always meet in the late hours
of early morning."
"I guess for some it would be strange?"
I said, "I can't sleep tonight,
maybe because of poetry,
or maybe out of old habit."
God said, "I couldn't sleep tonight,
maybe because of old habit."
"God, I read some Mark Twain tonight,
he was a great writer."
God said, "I used to visit him at night,
and I was with him when he wrote Huckleberry Finn."
I said, "How about Joan of Arc?"
"I was there, too."
I said, "I kinda knew."
God said, "Don't get me wrong,
I didn't write Huck or Joan,
just made sure the light was bright."
I said, "I wish that I could have a bright light."
"You always will as long as you want."
I said, "Thanks."
He said, "What's with the Gregorian Chants?"
I said, "I like the Chants,
it reminds me of you,
and when I was a little boy.
Everything was pure
the long white candles
and kneeling on the hard kneelers
Priests spoke words that calmed my soul.
And the Nuns
with their Rosary Beads,
how the sound of the Beads could be heard.
How there were magical secrets in the mass.
I loved the stories of the Prophets
And heroes of the Bible.

I loved Latin even though I couldn't understand,
it had magical power."
God said, "It had a certain magic."
I said, "I was just a boy
And knew nothing of war
or hunger.
I knew nothing of how men could hurt each other
and pray for your approval."
God said, "I do take issue with that,
to justify war and think I side with either of the mad armies."
"I heard once when I was a boy,
that there are no atheists in a foxhole."
God said, "Many strong prayers come from fear."
I said, "I know,
once I laid in a ditch and
begged your name."
God smiled, "You were just a boy."
"Didn't know I was a boy at the time.
I was scared and everything was burning
and the earth was shaking."
God said, "Your soul was shaking more than the earth."
I said, "Gregorian Chants remind me of
how the priest would lift the chalice of wine
and drink.
How his hands reached high almost grasping the cloak of heaven."
God said, "You're really serious tonight."
I said, "Maybe I am,
and I'd much rather talk of how Twain made fun of General Grant
at a banquet and how he made fun out of Emerson.
I think that's how life should be,
and how Grant laughed,
but Emerson didn't find any humor."
God said, "I know what's on your mind."
I said, "I know you do,
it's my friend, Trooper."
God said, "I promise he'll be alright."
I said, "Thanks."

If Jesus is Your Friend, You Still Shouldn't Tell People to Stick their Heads in a Bucket Of Shit and Pull Out Your Dong While Spinning in a Circle While Standing on a Barstool

"Fabs, how's it going?"
"Same old shit, a different day."
I said, "Heard you got barred from Wagner's."
"Yeah, Doris barred me again."
"How long this time?"
He said, "For life."
I said, "She's barred you for life at least ten times.
What'd you do this time?"
He said, "I was drinking the ignorant oil
and stood up on a barstool
and yelled at her
that Jesus is my friend
and if she don't like it, she can stick her red head
in a big bucket of shit."
I said, "That doesn't sound too bad,
and shouldn't get you barred for life."
He said, "Yeah, but while I was standing on the barstool
the guys started to spin me in a circle
and I pulled it out
and sort of flashed the whole bar."
I said, "Well, the Jesus being your friend
and her red head stuck in a bucket of shit isn't too bad.
But the spinning around in a circle
with your dong out flashing the bar is kind of a drum roll."
He said, "I guess I'll be on sit down for at least a week
but she'll calm down.
I'll buy her some chocolates
and maybe a pint of vodka,
that should loosen her grip."
I said, "Maybe,
but you've got to quit pulling your dong out

every time you get sauced."
He said, "I know,
but I kind of think it's pretty
and think everybody should get to look at it."
I said, "I'll tell her that you're sorry
and you didn't mean to flash the bar
and it just kind of fell out
because you were really dizzy from spinning
in a circle and
you didn't actually pull it out
and when it kind of fell out
you were holding it like a tightrope walker's pole
so you wouldn't fall."
He said, "Thanks, Dog."
I said, "The bucket of shit and
sticking her head in the bucket is on you."
He said, "After I give her the chocolates and
pint of vodka I'll tell her
that Jesus said for her to forgive me."
I said, "Enjoy your sit down time."

I Ain't Buying that Slushy for You, You Little Motherfucker

I was blessed to be with the sinners
that are going straight to hell on a Silver Glide toboggan.
The woman walked to the back of the gas station
where they had the crappy black coffee
yesterday's doughnuts and the sticky soda machine.
She was with a fat chubby kid who was about seven years
on this earth maybe eight
not much more
and maybe less.
He wore baggy shorts half way below his dirty knees
his chubby ass cheeks exposed
fat round legs bowed out and
yet his knees knocked
and he had high-top filthy tennis shoes
one dirty sock lower than the other
he was proudly sporting a Steelers black and gold t-shirt
he had a fat round face
and a short haircut like he had mange
and my best guess that she cut his hair to save a couple of bucks.
I watched as he grabbed a piggy cup
and started to fill it with cherry slushy.
The woman who I believe to be his mom
cuffed him on his ear and said,
"I ain't buying that slushy for you,
you little Motherfucker.
I hope you got some fuckin' money,
I ain't fuckin' paying for it."
He yelled, "I gots some money!"
Fate would have it that they then got behind me
in the checkout line
and I turned and looked down at the fat kid,
"You listen to your mother?"
He said, "Ah huh."
She said, "He don't ever listen."
I said, "I would have guessed."

I paid for my gas
walked out the door
and thought of William Carlos
about the purple plums
how he ate them and left a note.
I thought that this fat knock-kneed kid
with his ass cheeks hanging out doesn't have a chance
unless somehow he can hit a ball like Babe Ruth
or maybe he can become a cop.
I thought a slushy isn't really that important
and maybe I should have offered to pay
for the cherry slushy
but it really runs much deeper
and cooler
than purple plums eaten by any poet that would leave a note.

It's Not the Enema,
It's the Fear of the Enema

She handed me a cup of coffee,
"You were having a nightmare again."
I said, "I know."
"You were screaming
and you were kicking
and punching."
"I can't control my dreams."
"You kicked me hard in my leg
and it's all black and blue."
"I'm sorry,
I didn't mean to kick you."
"Were you dreaming about the bags again?"
"Yeah, it's always the bags
and they're chasing me.
And my brothers and sisters are standing
just like the von Trapp family
singing *The Hills Come Alive With The Sound of Music*
and pointing
standing on the steps singing that awful enema song,
'*Enema enema enema
enema bag new ... enema bag
for Y-O-U*'
And I'm running down the steps
out the kitchen door
through the big iron gate
and down the alley.
I'm running fast
and then there are enema bags everywhere
and the red enema bags are chasing me
and the enemas are singing
'*Hey mister black part
play a tune for me,*'
and I'm running bare ass
jumping over garbage cans
and over fences

and running
and I try to climb a big tree
but one of the enema bags grabs my leg
ties my leg up with a hose
then a stampede of enema bags are after me
and I can't get away
and the bags are squirting at my bare ass
then insult to injury
there's about twelve girls from Immaculate Conception
in their black and white oxfords
coming from the school carrying their books
with their uniforms rolled up
Leslie and Jackie with the round fanny
and there's Anna the cute Italian girl
and I'm in love with Anna
and she sees the enema bags and
she laughs
and all the other girls laugh
and start to cheer like a football cheer
when you want your team to score a touchdown
and kick their legs high
and I can almost see their underpants
and they're cheering for the enema bags and
I'm screaming
and screaming and
then I wake up."
She asked, "Your mother gave you a lot of enemas
when you were a little boy?"
I sipped my coffee, "I guess, but I was never sick."

First Pride, Then the Fall

I don't know what makes a
man fall from grace,
usually the fall is unseen by the fallen,
they usually hit the ground hard
and spend the remainder of their lives trying to get up.
I don't know why
I'm thinking of Jacob's ladder,
a climb from earth to heaven.
I'm drinking a cup of strong coffee
and thinking of my friend who was a Chief of Police.
A good man
honorable to a fault
church-going man that loves his God
and feared the flames of hell.
Because I spoke with him
knew of his fears and love
and saw in his eyes an emptiness
almost like he had no more tears to shed
for I'm sure as there is treachery
he often cried alone as if he were in a garden awaiting betrayal.
I think sometimes men fall from a ladder
because the ladder is too high
and in the fear of height they lose their footing.
Sometimes the rung of the ladder
is slick and their foot slips.
Sometimes the rung of the ladder breaks
and they fall.
Sometimes men are trying to get past them
and they climb up your back
step on your neck
smash your fingers
and it's hard to hold onto a ladder with crushed fingers.
Sometimes you are tossed down
by the Gods
all in the name of hubris.
It has been said often

by greater men,
"First pride, then the Fall."
I have fallen often
sometimes because of a slip
and often,
too often, I've been pushed
or tossed.
It matters not the fall
as much the tumult and awful sound.
I sounded like a big bag of shit thumping down
hitting hard on the ground.
But then the question,
"How high the bounce?"
That can only be measured by the height of the climb
equally proportionate to the fall,
almost like measuring action to the reaction.
But a bag of shit almost always makes
the same sound of an awful thud.
Now what makes a fall so hard is
when others are tossed down with you
and often those also tossed down land on you
kind of like you become their pillow,
which, of course, softens their fall.
Sometimes I drink strong coffee
just to stay awake
so that I don't dream of ladders like Jacob.
Guess maybe I just want my feet on the ground
and just tired of helping up good honorable men.
I'm just tired of seeing the empty eyes
of men praying in gardens
with crushed fingers.

Just Me and The Boys Having Fun

She said, "You think you're Charles Bukowski,
don't you?"
I said, "No, I don't."
"Yes, you do."
I said, "I don't even try to think I'm Bukowski."
She said, "You sit around in a dirty t-shirt
belch real loud
fart real loud
scratch yourself real loud
sit in your room real loud
type poems real loud
talk to yourself real loud
laugh to yourself real loud
and you're quiet real loud."
I said, "Farting and belching are better out,
and I don't talk to myself real loud
and you shouldn't be listening to my quiet
even when it's done real loud."
She said, "I can't help but listen,
your quiet is loud,
or sometimes you're mad real loud
like crazy real loud."
I asked, "Crazy real loud?"
She said, "Like when you're writing poetry,
I can hear you barking
and singing strange songs
and swearing
even cursing at God."
I said, "First of all, you shouldn't be listening.
Secondly, barking is healthy.
And even a shrink would tell you that singing alone
is just cleansing the soul.
And even Mark Twain swore.
And I'm not swearing at God,
I'm talking to God, which is different."
She said, "You do swear at God,

I've heard you.
In fact, you swear and shake your fist towards heaven."
I said, "God doesn't like sissies,
and He's tired of everyone asking for the same stupid stuff, like
"God, I need money,
and, God, if I get this promotion,
God, help me with my screwed-up kids,
help me
help me
help me."
God hates the begging and the whining.
In fact, God told me that He's tired of your shit, too."
She said, "God never told you He's tired of me."
I said, "Yes, He did,
in fact, God said you should do more stuff for me.
Like fix me a sandwich,
and God said there's never such a thing as too much mayo."
She said, "God never said that,
but I'll fix you a sandwich anyway."
I said, "I don't think I'm Bukowski,
I'm better than him.
He had limitations,
women
the drinking
racetrack
fighting.
He never had war,
real war,
fire and the smell.
He never had drugs,
heroin and cocaine,
men with gangrene and pregnant women with AIDS.
He never had to bury a whore
tell a grandfather that his grandson had been shot
and died on the dirty sidewalks.
He never had to lie and hold a woman's hand who lost love.
He never had to cut the rope of the hanged
He never had to wake up in the middle of the night sweating
hearing the hammer of a gun fall.

He never had to measure the dead.
I sometimes swear with God
and we both love the dirty words.
Sometimes, we bark together,
because we love to pretend we're dogs.
Sometimes, we pretend we're horses,
and sometimes we're birds.
Sometimes, me and God pretend we're snakes
and we coil ourselves around each other and laugh
like we're monkeys.
Sometimes me and God even cry together,
I wipe His tears,
and He wipes mine.
Sometimes, me and God fall asleep together,
and guess what … we both snore.
Sometimes, we invite Bukowski to our party,
and that old bastard shows up drunk.
But we all get along
and he reminds me that he had a 'typer' that
made cash,
and for me, it's okay to try."
She said, "You better take your medicine.
I'll fix the sandwich."
I said, "You can put monkey meat on it,
and easy on the baby seal sauce."
She said, "You're crazy."
I said, "So was Mozart,
Van Gogh, and Nietzsche,
and guess what … we all talk with God."
She said, "That's nice."
I said, "Next week we're planning to all go out and visit a whorehouse,
and you're not invited."
She said, "I'll get you some soup with the sandwich."
I said, "Not too hot,
the guys hate to burn their lips."
I went into the room and told the guys,
"I better not mention Harpo or she'll think I'm really crazy."
The guys said, "Shouldn't have mentioned the whorehouse.

I hope she makes tomato soup
with roasted red peppers,
we're tired of chicken noodle."
I said, "Let's get busy and write,
because somewhere there's a guy making a nuke
and twisting the bolts too tight."
They both said, "Yep, twisting the bolts too tight."
We could hear the wrench fall,
and Satan cackled real
real loud.

Murder on Christmas Eve

We had a warrant for Weasel
for killing Valerie on a Christmas Eve.
He and some other Motherfucker shot
the car up about thirty-four times.
Bullets went through the trunk of the car
through the back seat
and struck Valerie in her back.
A through-and-through wound
through the heart.
Her last words were,
"I'm hit."
She slumped over and died.
Witnesses said they knew it was a gun.
It was loud,
and it sounded just like a
freight train.
I knew her brother
and her grandfather.
Her brother was her twin
his name was Sammy
and her grandfather's name was Harry.
I spoke with Harry
and he cried and said,
"Get them,
they killed my baby."
Weasel was seventeen years old
and thought himself an 'O.G.' — Original Gangster
wanted to make himself a name.
By the way, I almost forgot,
Valerie had a two-year-old son at home
and this makes me sad that he'd never know his mother.
I arrested Weasel
and convicted him of 1st Degree Murder.
He was given a Life Sentence.
Later, the conviction was overturned … because
because
because … of overambitious men.

I watched as the law distorted truth.
Weasel said, "I didn't mean to kill anyone.
The thirty-four bullets were only meant to scare people,
not really to harm nobody."
So, it wasn't like he was really aiming to kill anyone.
He was just spraying the car with hot lead
or confetti
or rice that you throw at weddings
or maybe like a baseball that you throw underhand
for a little boy to catch
or like when you throw a toddler up in the air
and catch him when he giggles
or even when you might push a kid on a swing
on a warm summer day and his little feet reach high for the clouds.
Weasel shot the guns just like that,
just like confetti
wedding rice
throwing a baseball underhand
or tossing a giggling toddler
or pushing a kid on a swing.
The bullets were nothing like a freight train
but maybe more like a Christmas Eve snow.
Weasel got out of jail about the
same time that Valerie's son would be old enough
to ask questions about important things,
like little girls
and more questions about little girls.
You know, his little voice was changing
and he was getting taller
and was just at the height when a little boy notices
and asks questions about little girls.
Every so often, the little boy around Christmas
asks, "Was my mom pretty?"
And Great-Grand Pappy Harry says,
"Just like the Christmas Angel on top of the tree."

Surveillance

Sitting in a D-car alone
in any place you don't belong
watching the morning sun rise
and the junkies arrive like black birds.
Crouched low in the seat your head just peaking
over the steering wheel
trying to catch a glimpse of a license plate.
Etching the numbers on the palm of your hand
knowing that you can later lick the ink off
like a forgivable sin or spit it out of your mouth like a hair.
Always and always a reason,
why the juice
the oil
skag
junk
because I lost my job
my brother died
my girl broke up with me
my father beat me
my mother left me when I was two
and ran off without me
leaving me with loneliness.
Reason to steal
and lie
beat
rob
hurt
always learning to make promises
and break the dreams
a thousand pieces of broken hearts
and always being able to cry on cue
like turning on a rusty faucet
in some filthy bathroom in some Godforsaken place
and it's always for the rush
the jolt
a thousand Christmas'

a million fireworks shot in the sky
spoon and cotton
and fire it up baby
and no longer shame
no longer dream
or hope
only the needle and the damage
always the hustle
and every day is spent chasing the fix.
War on drugs my ass
it was lost long ago
on the streets.
But if you can touch the soul of the junkman
you will find that something was important
maybe a teacher that fluffed his hair
or a toy that was wound up
or maybe a coin
or a ballgame where he spilled ketchup on the dog
or maybe a birthday candle that was blown out by granny
or maybe a lover's kiss that faded like a cloud across the moon
or maybe a sister that believed in him
or mother that smiled before she breathed her last breath
or a father that laid beside him in bed and snored.
And always sitting in a D-car
looking for anything …
anything at all
anything that can keep your heart from turning to stone.

Street Justice

Willie Wilson was a great boxer.
A black nappy kid from Braddock
who was blacker than smoke gone from the steel mills,
and as they say, black smoke on a hot July day.
Willie almost made the Olympics,
he was that good,
so smooth,
all glide.
Just a magic man on canvas,
all leather and silk.
A born champion made from dreams
on the poor side of town.
We wanted to call him *Whip Willie Wilson,*
but he said,
"My fight name is Silky Smooth Wilson."
He said he didn't like to be called Willie,
because, he said,
"It sounds like a wet fart going through corduroy."
But Willy was silk smooth and won a TV title
and should have been at least a millionaire,
but it wasn't in the cards.
But I'll tell you true,
he once had the lights.
I remember the night he won the title,
he was all peacock proud
and wore his belt for weeks.
I saw him in a Denny's restaurant,
he was sporting his belt and mouthing to the waitress,
just like Ali,
"I'm the greatest,
I'm better than best and smoother than silk."
But that was long ago
before he started to shoot heroin.
He lost a ten rounder to a stumble bum,
and did most of his training in slop joints
and that was the beginning of the end.

I don't know who gave him the oil,
but it took away all the magic
and the lights.
Returning to the streets which he never really had left,
caught a couple decisions beating the dope man,
and started to rob for the feel good.
Trouble finds trouble,
he hooked up with Jimmy "Slack in the Ass" Jenkins,
a plank of a man who did snatch and grab,
mostly old lady Bingo money,
car doors unlocked petty thefts.
He tried a little boosting selling stolen meat from a garbage bag,
an Auto Theft moment ...
a stolen car with a high speed chase,
and it finally did him a little sit down time.
Like I said, trouble finds trouble
Silky and Slack in the Ass
decided to rob Neal's Bar.
They snuck in the side of the bar
and went to the second floor.
While they were robbing
they had heavy feet and Old Man Neal heard and met them
as they were walking out with his TV ...
The rules changed:
First rule: Don't rob a man that's holding a gun.
Second rule: The man with the gun makes the rules.
Old Man Neal was holding the gun,
to be exact, a twelve gauge shotgun.
Neal knew both the boys
and pointed his shotgun and said,
"You boys want to put my TV back?"
They both said, "Sure enough, Mister Neal."
Mister Neal said, "Now you boys get."
They started to walk towards Mister Neal
hoping to get out the door,
but Mister Neal wasn't taking any chances and
pointed the shotgun high.
Third rule:
Any confusion, go back to the Second rule:

"No, you boys ain't leaving the way you came,
you boys can leave out the window."
Holding the aim of the shot gun at them he said,
"Now you boys go ahead and get."
Slack in the Ass opened the second floor window
and was the first to jump.
He landed like a thud of a heavy bag of shit
on the hard cobblestone street
and broke both his legs.
Then Silky Smooth jumped
and he landed on Slack in the Ass,
cushioning his jump.
But I want you to know that Silky was kind of a good man,
and had some street loyalty,
so he dragged Slack in the Ass
to the Emergency Room with two broken legs.
He told them, "Slack in the Ass
was hit by a big Buick and he can testify."
It was a pretty good street lie,
and documented on the hospital chart,
and it even made the second page news:
Man Hit by Buick.
I got two arrest warrants for Silky and
Slack in the Ass for Second Story Burglary.
Old Man Neal decided that he didn't want to press charges
and felt that justice was served.
I filed the paper in the back of the unfounded
but used the unfounded possibility as a threat,
to kind of slow the boys down just a little tad.
This was years ago and we're all much older and wiser,
and we kind of learn from the hard thud of experience.
Slack in the Ass' legs are bowed and he walks with a cane.
Silky Smooth ain't so smooth anymore and drinks bottom shelf
whiskey, and only has the retold stories.
But I'll tell you true,
he once was smooth as silk and had the lights
and that ain't too bad even on a bad day.

Art of the Jockey Strap

Not many people know
and most would be afraid to ask
but not my friend Yoeeee Girl
because she ain't afraid of nothin' and
she asked, "Can you tell me about putting on a jockey strap?"
I said, "What?"
She said, "Can you tell me about putting on a jockey strap?"
I said, "Whatda ya mean?"
"Is there an art or
a manual for teaching a man to putting on a jockey strap?"
I said, "Well, I don't think there's a manual but
I'm sure it's an art."
Yoeeee asked, "Well, how is it an art?"
I said, "Well, it's kind of a rite of passage
handed down, I think, from the Greeks.
It's an art taught by a father to his son
or grandfather to his grandson
or maybe by a priest or rabbi handed down.
It's like a Bar Mitzvah or a Confirmation or
when a boy is taught to go hunting in the woods alone
or taught to drive a car
or first cigar
or first beer
or learns to tie a necktie
or when a boy first kisses a girl.
Kinda an unspoken passage."
She asked, "What do you mean?"
"Well, when a boy is given his first jockey strap
he's recognized as a young man.
You see, it's the first time that he grows peach fuzz
on his little walnuts and the father must tell him
all the important things."
"What kind of important things?"
I said, "Well, for one, how to put it on."
"Ok. I'm all ears, tell me."
"First thing you got to learn

is that the little pouch goes in the front.
Because many an unschooled boy would
put the pouch in the back
and kinda look like a horse pulling a junk wagon.
The second thing is that the boy would be taught
to sit down and put the jockey strap on
and make sure that he don't get caught on his foot.
Because if you get the jockey strap caught on your foot
you can be launched just like an arrow.
I mean the strength of a jockey strap can fire you maybe
eighteen or twenty feet into the air
just like an arrow.
And even if you're sitting on a chair
you can be launched head over heels.
My father told me that he was at the lyceum
with my Uncle Benny and my uncle was standing up
on one foot at a time, kind of hopping.
Well, he caught his foot in the strap
and *Ping*
he was shot maybe twenty-five feet in mid-air
straight out the second story window and
landed in a rosebush with the strap over his ears.
But thank God for the rosebush
because that's what broke his fall
and he wasn't hurt too bad,
except for a few thorns
and his pride.
I mean he was butt ass
sitting and had to be pulled out of the bush.
A few girls were there when he came crashing through the window
and were giggling when they pulled him free.
But Uncle Benny denied it was him
and said it was my Uncle Bernie,
but it makes no difference more than fleas on a hound,
it's still one hell of a rite of passage.
I guess if I was to best make you understand
it's like when a little girl wears her first training bra.
I mean a mother or a grandmother

got to tell her about
the floppinstoppin, and that's a similar passage."
Yoeeee Girl said,
"Did I ever tell you sometimes you're a dumbbell?"
I said, "Not really, just when I'm asked dumb questions."

Reason behind Reason not to Lift the Seat

There is a reason behind
the reason but sometimes I just make shit up.
My girlfriend was really mad
at me because I peed
on the toilet seat.
She said, "Didn't your mother teach
you anything?
You're such a little pig.
I'm tired of you peeing on the seat
all you have to do is lift it up
and put it down.
Up
down
up
down.
Is that so hard?"
I sat down and lowered my head,
"There's a reason that I don't lift the seat.
I know if I tell you
you'll just make fun and laugh at me."
She said, "Oh, this aught to be good,
I got to hear the reason."
"You wouldn't believe me
and will only laugh."
"No-no, I got to hear the reason,
this aught to be good."
"Alright," I said,
"When I was just a little shaver,
I came running into the house
because I had to pee,
and we weren't allowed to pee in the alley.
I was really in a hurry,
not only because I didn't want to pee my pants
but it was a summer day and
I wanted to stay outside and play.
Well, I was in such a hurry,

I flung the toilet seat up
with one swoop
and at the same time pulled out my little handle.
The toilet seat went up
came down
and slammed shut on my little Skippy.
I fell back, hit my head on the tub
and was dizzy.
I remember crying
and running to my mom with my little shorts
wrapped around my ankles.
My mother swooped me up,
"What happened?"
Crying real tears I said, "The toilet seat bit me."
She said, "My goodness."
"Then, insult to injury,
I got the whipping of my life,
now don't laugh.
In my own little innocent way I said
to my mom,
'*Kiss it.*'
and being my shorts were already down
my mom beat my little ass pink.
And that's why
I don't sometimes pick up the toilet seat."
My girlfriend said,
"You're such a jerk
and your pants are on fire and your nose is growing."
I grit my teeth smiling and said,
"Well, most of it's true,
except the parts I made up.
Like the little pink bottom part but it
was the best reason without denying at the moment that I could think of.
I could have blamed it on a dog
or a wino."
She said, "Just lift the seat."
Again I lowered my head
and pretended shame,

"Okay,
up down
up down.
Think I got it now?
Up
down
up
down."
She said, "Oh God, your poor mother."
I asked, "Are we done here,
and can I go out and play?"

Pinhead the Fireman

I was sitting with Pinhead
drinking a beer.
He'd just retired from the fire department
after twenty-five years.
I asked him, "Did you ever put out a fire?"
He said, "No, but I started a few."
I said, "Every man to his own poison."
He said, "Sometimes I miss the action."
I said, "Well, light your house up
and fall through the burning floor.
It will bring back memories."
He said, "No, really, sometimes I miss the heat.
Sirens and running into the flames."
I said, "Are you crazy?"
He said, "It's hard to explain
unless you had the heat."
I said, "You miss stealing from the unfortunate
people that watch everything go up in flames."
He said, "I remember an old guy
that came walking back to the truck.
Smoke all over his face and
his legs were clinking.
Clink ... clink ... clink.
Inside his rubber boots
were two bottles of whiskey"
"What did you do?"
He said, "Nothing.
I thought about telling the Captain,
but then you're labeled a snitch."
"Whatever happened to the guy?"
"He went away some place in a puff of smoke
and then he retired and died."
I said, "Any regrets?"
"Just a couple.
Should have shared the whiskey."
He looked a thousand miles away.

"Yeah, wish I could have stopped …
a couple of our guys that walked into the final alarm,
when everything came crashing down.
I knew the girl,
Conway … she was pretty … two others.
Nobody's fault …
they died for no good reason."
I said, "Some things you have no control over."
Pinhead ordered another beer.
"One time I saved a couple of kids on the third floor,
if that counts for anything."
I said, "It counts, just like the guy that took the bottles of whiskey.
It all counts."

A Whore's Story

On a bad night there was a crack whore
that I arrested for trying to sell her pussy.
She tried to run
fought for a quick minute
kicking
and punching
swearing
and screaming.
An Italian girl
olive skin
brown eyes
and black silk hair.
She sat in the back of the D-car
crying almost to a sob.
She begged for freedom
and said, "I'm just trying to support a habit,
I don't rob or steal."
I ain't murdered anybody.
I just sell my ass.
Let me go ... please."
I told her,
"Listen, it's your turn,
nothing personal.
You'll be out before I finish the report."
She said, "I'm on probation."
I said, "Ouch."
"If you let me go," she said, "I'll blow you for nothing."
"I don't think my Sergeant will let me get blown.
In fact, I'm sure it's against rules and regulations.
Specifically stating:
Blow jobs will tarnish the badge ... Section #69-101
No Blow Jobs for the men.
No Johnsons.
No Head.
No Cleaning the Rust from the Old Pipes.
I mean, it's all written in black and white.

Sorry."
She cried some more
and we took her to the station.
We gave her coffee
and a cigarette.
(Police will always give you coffee
and a cigarette even if you're not allowed to blow them.)
I asked her, "Why are you walking the streets?"
She said, "I sell my ass for oil."
I said, "Go to the clinic and dry out."
"I'm afraid of hospitals," she took a long drag from the
cigarette, "I had to get a hysterectomy because
some freak broke a light bulb inside of me."
I said, "What?"
"Some sick freak broke a light bulb inside of me
and I bled real bad, almost died."
"What happened to the freak?"
"My brother killed him."
"Your brother killed the freak?"
She said, "I wasn't walking the streets then,
or supporting a habit.
I was just a good Italian girl.
My brother defended my honor.
Stomped his brains out
and stuck a light bulb where the sun don't shine.
He was found guilty
and is serving life because of me.
Because of me, he kills a freak
defending my honor.
Pretty sad, isn't it?"
I said, "Honor is sometimes expensive."
She put the cigarette out,
"He's serving life and he
thinks I'm at home making pasta and planting tomatoes."
I whispered, " I wouldn't tell him.
Are you telling me the truth?"
She said, "I don't lie to cops."
I walked her to the door.
"Go home.

You got a get-out-of-jail-free card.
Give me a call sometime when you're making pasta."
She asked, "You letting me go?"
"Don't let the door hit you in your chubby Italian."
I watched as she walked into the night,
and thought … *Blow jobs are overrated, but*
they ain't too bad even on a bad night.

Never Go Fishing with a Lawyer

Never go fishing with a lawyer.
I mean never,
don't even think about it —
not ever, not even on a sunny day.
I have a good memory about some things,
and many things are sent to me as life lessons,
maybe by fate or by Divine Providence
or just simple laws of the universe … I don't know
for sure but sometimes fate collides with chance
and lightning strikes.
I can't remember the lawyer's name,
but I think it was Stanley Snodgrass
or maybe it was Hugo Hodgepodge
but it was something like Maury or Sid
I can't remember for sure.
So I'm going with my gut
and calling him Stanley Snodgrass
but it could have been Sid … Snodgrass.
Anyway, as I recall … Stanley
went out in a boat
and it got really dark
and the clouds gathered and were black
and there were great gusts of wind
that tossed the little boat
and the rain started to fall like it was poured from buckets.
I know this to be true because there
were other boats
and other fishermen
and all started to row to the safety of the shore.
Well, Stanley
stood up in the middle of the boat,
extended his arms,
and shouted, "Here I am, God!"
And no sooner than when he got
the word "God" out of his mouth
a lightning bolt came from the sky

and struck Stanley right on the top of his head.
Everyone that witnessed
saw Stanley explode.
And no sooner than after watching Stanley
blow up the sun came back out
and the lake was calm.
The only thing left of Stanley Snodgrass
were his shoes, which were smoking,
and his red tackle box.
All the other fishermen that witnessed
the explosion of Stanley
could only say,
"Wow! Stanley was just turned into toast."
Now I know there's a lesson here someplace,
just don't know what it is,
and don't know why anyone would
point themselves out to God during an electric storm.
Maybe it has something to do with the laws
of God and man
and hubris,
or maybe it has something to do with fishing.
And I can't help but wonder what kind of shoes Stanley wore,
and what ever happened to his red tackle box?
As for me ... I ain't ever going fishing with a lawyer,
and that ain't no fish tale, that's just a
lightning striking fact.

If you Need Glasses, All Black Men Sometimes Look Alike

I ain't sayin' he's blind,
all I'm sayin' is that I don't think
he could see too good.,
that's all I'm sayin'.
And the only reason I'm sayin' this is
because when we went to the pistol range
to qualify we'd have to pump in a couple
extra shots in his target so he'd qualify
because when he was shootin' he couldn't hit a bear
in the ass with a bass fiddle.
Smudge was a good dude
and he wasn't prejudiced or anything like that,
I never heard him ever use the N-word,
it's just he was born on the white side of the tracks.
I just think he was bat blind,
that's all I'm sayin'.
Now, he bought some heroin
from Easy Money
and eventually paper follows the crime
and Easy was picked up
cuffed
tossed
humbugged
printed and mugged
and his shackled feet made way to the big court.
Now Smudge went to court
raised his hand high to God
and swore to tell the truth
with the stern reminder of the last Great Day.
Smudge under oath told the court his
name and that he was workin' undercover
assigned to the Narcotics Unit
and that he had worked the streets
and knew shit the pants danger
and fear that reeks like the smell of a rat

under a back alley garbage can.
He told the judge that he
bought the do-bad from Easy Money
and that he had purchased it with marked money
and that he had greased the hand of Easy.
Smudge stated that the do-bad was
bagged and tagged and sent to the Crime Lab.
The magic machine tested the do-bad
and it came back positive for China White,
Drano, and Mister Clean.
The District Attorney, all proud
and puffed chest, "Detective, can you point
out Easy Money as the man who sold you the do-bad?"
Smudge, with a proud eye squint pointed,
"That's Easy, the black man
in the grey t-shirt and dew-rag
sitting next to the black man with the white shirt and tie."
The black man with the grey t-shirt and dew-rag
stood up and said,
"Detective, are you sure I sold you the do-bad?"
Smudge said clear as a church bell,
"I'm sure as the shine of my badge you sold me the do-bad."
"You're positive I sold you the
China White,
Drano, and
Mister Clean?"
"Sure as the sound of a cell door slamming."
Before the District Attorney could shout,
"Objection!"
The black man with the dirty grey t,-shirt and dew-rag
said, "Your Honor, I move that my client with the
white shirt and tie,
who is the real for real, Easy Money, be granted his freedom,
because the Detective clearly identified me as
the do-bad salesman and
further I want the Court to make note that
all black men don't look alike,
unless we're hunting for blind justice."
The judge pounded his hammer

and said, "The Detective identified
Malcolm Shazbam, the Defense Attorney, as the
do-bad salesman, and I don't believe that
Malcolm Shazbam sells do-bad.
Easy Money is free.
Now all of you get out of my house
before I change my mind.
And Malcolm, from now on you make sure you wear a tie,
and Detective, I'm ordering you to see an eye doctor
and take a sensitivity class.
Case Dismissed."

Just Say "Okey-Dokey"

Sometimes even if you tell the truth
nobody's going to believe you.
"Nasty" Cornelius had been coming to the gym for a quick minute
and had a couple of fights under his trunks.
He was an on and off fighter,
more on than off,
he had losses on bad decisions
and some wins on bad decisions,
depending on the lights and size of the card girls.
Anyway, it didn't matter much because
the gym was his cathedral
and the ring his confessional and
he was staying out of jail.
We called Cornelius "Nate" for short
but mostly everybody called him "Nasty".
"Nasty Nate" because
he'd always hit you below the belt.
It was just a bad habit
that was hard to break,
you know, like it's harder to get permission
than asking forgiveness.
Anyway, because of Nasty I'm now convinced
they should legalize marijuana.
You see, one day he was hitting the bag
and I came over to teach him how to sit
down on a punch.
In fact, I put a pair of trunks on the bag
so he'd learn to hit above the belt.
He had on a hooded sweatshirt
with a pouch in the front.
I told him,
"Nasty Nate, you've got to step to the left
and let your weight shift.
You've got to hit from your center,
slightly below the belly button."
I tapped him on his belly

and it was then I felt a lump in his sweatshirt.
I reached in and sure as blue sky
has a thundercloud
I pulled out a bag of weed.
I said, "What's this, a bag of oregano?"
Nasty said, quick as a low blow,
"It's not mine, coach, I'm holding it for a friend."
I took the weed, put it in my back pocket.
"Get dressed, Nasty,
you're out of the gym as of right now
and forever.
Do not pass go.
Adios, amigo.
Di di mau."
Nasty said, "For real, coach, the weed ain't mine."
I said, "Please, you're hurting my ears."
He walked back to the locker room
and a couple of the kids came running over.
"Come on, coach,
Nasty is part of the family.
You can't kick him out of the gym."
One kid said,
"He's probably telling the truth.
The weed probably was someone else's."
I snapped, "You must have been hit harder
than I thought.
Get back to jumping rope or you can help
carry his gym bag out the door."
Nasty walked slowly out of the locker room,
"Give me one more chance, coach."
I said, "Give me one good reason." He said,
"Because I'm like your son
and I ain't got no place to go."
I said, "I only asked for one good reason.
You can stay, but I'm going to have you pee
in a cup
every full moon and
you're on probation forever and one day.
Get back and get dressed

and it's your night to empty the spit bucket."
I locked the gym and
threw the marijuana in my glove compartment.
Two weeks later I was stopped by the police for
running a stop sign.
The man in blue asked for my driver's license and owner's card.
I opened the glove compartment and as sure as
a lie will follow a sin
the weed fell out and
what came out of my mouth was,
"It's not mine, officer. I'm holding it for a friend."

25 Reasons the Dog Quit Drinking

My friend Kenny Ken
always asks me, "Dog, why'd you stop drinking?"
We were partners in law and in crime
and he has the right to ask,
after all, we drank beer for more brags
and bottom shelf whiskey for more years than I can remember,
and I guess it's like that when two that were married to the ignorant oil,
one deserves an answer, as if it would make any difference.
I never told him, but after all these years
maybe, I guess, he deserves an answer of why
anyone would just go cold turkey
and stop drinking the suds.
After all, we rode in the same police car
and we were young detectives once,
and we covered each other when we were chasing the bad guys
and fought for truth
and rolled in the gutter for the sake of justice.

Well, Kenny Ken,
here is a list of the reasons why Dog quit drinking:

1: Instant asshole — just add alcohol.

2: Walls that I blocked with my fists.

3: Doors that I blocked with my fists.

4: Walls that I blocked with my head.

5: Doors that I blocked with my head.

6: Fists that I blocked with my head.

7: Bottles that I blocked with my head.

8: Times that I soiled my pants and asked, "Do farts have lumps?"

9: Discovering that farts don't have lumps.

10: Singing Karaoke.

11: Hoping some star struck agent discovers me when I sing karaoke.

12: Beer-bumps on my car.

13: Falling asleep with a blow-up doll at a red light and backing traffic on an early morning rush hour.

14: Driving drunk with an open bottle and a case of beer bought from a bar in Lawrenceville, with the blow-up doll, with hopes to reach Tampa Bay, Florida to see a woman, only sobering up in South Carolina.

15: Continuing to drive from South Carolina to Tampa Bay, Florida with a blow-up doll and a huge hangover, only to discover when you arrive in Tampa Bay that the woman has moved to Sydney, Australia.

16: Waking up one day not knowing where you are ... where your clothes are or where you parked your car ... don't have a clue how you got where you are or where you've been and waking up naked with a woman you don't know. Don't recognize the ceiling and you have a big cheese titty stuck in your mouth and have a beer boner.

17: Having the woman pull the big cheese titty with a sound of suck and pop that reverbs off the walls and you stand up in the middle of the bed with the beer boner and start to sing ... *"Everybody loves somebody sometime ... "* and still think you're in the bar entertaining a star struck agent.

18: The woman can't remember your name either.

19: Always-Always-Always a bunch of knobby head kids jumping on the bed after the titty is pulled from your mouth and you don't know their names either.

20: Always the headaches and lumps and you can't remember the doors, walls, or fists that you blocked the night before.

21: Waking up only to find that your wallet is gone and a bunch of no name knobby kids have a wad of money in their hands and the lady with no name says, "Don't you remember that you gave the knobby heads the money?" And then discover you parked your car in the middle of the neighbors lawn. The car door's open and the headlights are on … and to further the problem, you can't find the keys.

22: Unable to pay your rent or eat because you have no money in your wallet.

23: You start to smell like a big cheese titty.

24: You discover it's not the big cheese titty smell, it's the fart that had a lump that smells.

25: Even your blow-up doll hates you.

This is just a short list of the many reasons why the Dog quit drinking, but the number one reason that Dog quit he will never tell, and you'll just have to ponder and think about that for a lump in your pants moment. If you have any questions, just add alcohol and park our car in the middle of a neighbor's lawn and find a big cheese titty to suck.

Head in a Bowling Ball Bag

Blade was sentenced to life in Rahway Prison
with no hope for parole.
Some people should be behind bars forever
plus a day
and a day
and a day
and then some.
Blade got his name because he was always
cutting or
slicing
stabbing
knifing
daggering
sticking
another human being.
Blade was on parole when he did his last stabbing
and in his mind he was just defending his cellmate's —
Yellow Wolf's — honor.
Yellow Wolf was serving time awaiting parole
and he asked his friend Blade,
"My woman hasn't come to see me in months.
When you get out, can you check on her
and find out why she ain't been around to see me?"
Blade said, "I'll look out, and we cool."
Blade got out and took a train to New York with his nephews
and went to all the good places in the Big Apple
Empire State Building
Times Square
Madison Square Garden.
Even took a walk through Central Park
and he took his nephews for rides on the subways
ate New York pizza
and hot pretzels.
Then he remembered his promise to Yellow Wolf
and took a cab to Queens to see why the woman forgot
to visit Yellow Wolf and show her love.

Blade and his nephews found her apartment,
and when she answered the door, Blade asked,
"Why ain't you been around to see Yellow Wolf?"
He then heard from the bedroom,
"Who in the fuck wants to know?"
Blade then knew,
"Baby, Yellow Wolf loves you
and you disrespecting and spreading your ass."
Then a big Red-Headed Viking
stepped from the bedroom wearing Yellow Wolf's bathrobe,
"Tell Yellow Wolf there's a new conductor riding the train,
and get your asses out before
I put my foot deep in your inquiry."
Blade said, "Very disrespectful."
With a quick swish, pulled out his pig sticker
and lunged ten inches deep into the heart of the Viking.
Before the Viking could utter Leif Erickson,
Blade cut his throat twice and
stabbed him six more times,
and whispered in his ear,
"So much for your foot, Motherfucker."
Then he grabbed Yellow Wolf's woman,
"I should cut out your hot box
but that would make Yellow Wolf cry.
Bitch, this is your fault
so you're gonna help cool down your cheating ass.
Get me a couple of suitcases
and garbage bags."
Turning to his nephews,
"Let's put this Viking into the tub.
I got to perform some surgery."
They dragged the Viking and Yellow Wolf's
blood-stained bathrobe into the tub.
Blade cut the Viking into several pieces,
arms
legs
feet
hands
belly

and off with his big red head.
He stuffed his legs and arms in a suitcase
and his belly into a garbage bag
and his big red head into a bowling ball bag.
He then told the woman, "Keep quiet
or you'll disappear in pieces."
And he then took her car keys,
"You can pick your car up the police pound on Monday."
Blade then took the Viking around to different dumpsters
and tossed him around the city to include
sewers for legs and arms
and feet into the Hudson.
He told his nephews, "Get rid of the bowling ball bag
with the big red head,"
and let them out at the bus terminal,
"I'll see you back in Pittsburgh."
The nephews took the bag
and decided to place the Viking's head in a locker.
The problem was the bag was dripping blood
and a police officer saw the blood puddle.
The nephews were arrested.
Both sung like canaries
and Uncle Blade was arrested.
Blade showed no remorse
and the hammer of justice fell his ass back to Rahway.
Turned out the Viking had a guard who was his best friend
and, after a couple of months, the guard approached Blade.
Guard asked, "You killed my best friend,
and I've got to ask you how could a human being do this to
another human being?"
Blade looked up at the guard,
"I'll answer your question if you can answer mine first."
The Guard said, "Fair. Ask your question."
Blade said, "It's a two-part question.
First, did you go to the Viking's funeral?"
Guard said, "He was my best friend.
Yes, I went to his funeral."
Blade asked, "Well, tell me, was he buried in one box,
or was he buried in several little boxes?"

Wrong as a Shit Sandwich with Cold Gravy

Issy actually followed the blood trail to the hospital
and I went to the station to talk with the actor.
When I first saw him
a shackle was on his leg
and it was connected to a steel ring on the floor.
I introduced myself
read him his rights and
asked him, "You understand your rights?"
He said, "Yeah, I don't have to talk with you?"
I said, "Till you talk with a lawyer."
He said, "I don't need a lawyer if you keep it real."
I said, "I'll keep it real."
He said, "I only hit him once."
I asked, "Only once?"
He said, "Alright, a couple of times."
"Well, you hit him hard enough to knocked his dick in the dirt
and he's turning cold and they might have to tag his toe."
He said, "It was a fair one
and he lost."
I said, "Want to explain fair?"
He said, "Mano-Mano.
Him against me.
Just two rams on a hill butting heads."
I said, "Your head must be harder."
He said, "The guy stole my Benjamin's
and he was trying to ram jam my wife and
he was telling my wife I was alley-catting around on her.
And unfortunately the motherfucker got caught,
that's all
nothing more
nothing less.
Just two rams butting heads."
I said, "Just so my Sergeant understands,
just two rams on a hill butting heads and
he was stealin' your Benjamin's
trying to ram-jam your woman

and talking shit on you?"
He said, "Yeah, and unfortunately he's unfortunate."
I asked, "Can you fill in the blanks?"
He said, "He worked for me
and I caught him with his hand in the cookie jar
but that's okay cause I always leave a couple extra cookies
for the rats.
But he tried to put his fingerprints where they don't belong
and if you touch fire sometimes you get burned."
I asked, "He touch fire and he get burned?"
He said, "Nebnose was trying to look
under my woman's wedding gown and got burnt.
And if I'm correct it's
marked Confidential: For My Eyes Only.
And you know the rules:
you can't look
and you can't touch."
I said, "I know the rules."
He said, "Then while he was dropping bait,
he tells the mother of my children
that I was castin' bait for Eda."
I asked, "Who's Eda?"
He said, "Brown Sugar woman,
church-going Eda with the high ass.
Now, it's bad enough Nebnose trying to sneak a peak but
he's running his lips on me about Eda and
that's wrong as a shit sandwich with cold gravy."
I said, "I understand.
But let's see if I got it right for the Sergeant.
A man shouldn't steal cookies and
you caught Nebnose trying to sneak a peek
and he shit-mouthed you about
Brown Sugar Eda with the high ass?"
He said, "'Zactly, and I tested his jaw."
I said, "Makes sense to me,
if you neb where you don't belong
sometimes you get headbutted.
Anything else?"
"Yeah, can you loosen the shackle?

'cause I ain't going to run."
I got the turnkey
and dropped the empty shackle to the floor,
"I knows you wouldn't run 'cause
any man that wouldn't eat a shit sandwich with cold gravy
is as true as the menu in a slop joint
and quite incapable of lying to the cook."
He said, "Thanks for keeping it real"
I said, "Sure."

Amonti is Told the Secret, But He Just Forgot

I guess some things just make you sad,
and there are many disappointments.
Maybe success is measured by the height of the fall
and how some men pull themselves up by their laces.
I've seen many sunny days,
but the days when the cold winds cut
and rains drench the bones
all seem to hurt the body as I've grown older.
I was watching the News
and the reporter told of four men that were arrested
for distribution and trafficking of large amounts of heroin
and cocaine
thousands of dollars seized
many guns
AK-47 Assault Rifle
9mm
45cal
AR-15
lots of ammo
enough ammo to start a small war.
I've seen this many times,
more times than I can count or remember,
but always the disappointment …

Many years ago a small boy by the name of Amonti
was no bigger than a minute,
all wide-eyed sunshine.
I remember like it was yesterday
and believed that youth would last forever.
I took a team of young boxers to Indianapolis
the Black Expo
to fight in the Muhammad Ali Tournament.
We had breakfast with the *Great One*
and he signed everything from hats
to gloves
and he even signed little kids' heads.

We spent three days in the ring
winning and losing
eating well and
living fat.
It was the greatest.
To show appreciation, the Pittsburgh Team
bought a bicycle to give to Ali,
because that was the reason he became a boxer.
Young Cassius came crying to a police officer
and wanted to beat the kid who stole his bike.
The policeman's name was Joe Martin, and
he said, "Alright, if you want to beat the kid up,
you first better learn to box."
And the magic began:
Float like a butterfly.
and sting like a bee
and the next thing he wins the Olympic Gold
and Sonny Liston is flat on his back
and Walcott counts him out.
Anyway, we had the bicycle and
decided that we'd give the bike to Ali
so he could give it away to a kid.
I picked Amonti to give the bike,
"Amonti, you're the youngest,
get in the ring with Ali and give him the bicycle."
Amonti started to walk up with the bodyguards,
then got scared and started to cry and ran back into my arms,
"I can't do this coach.
I'm afraid."
The bodyguard asked,
"You want to go up with him coach?"
I said, "Yes," and almost ran Amonti over getting into the ring.
Muhammad Ali was bigger than a small boy's dream
and he took the bike and asked, looking down at Amonti,
"Did you steal my bicycle?"
Amonti looked up at Ali and said,
"I didn't steal your bike."
Ali said, "I think you stole my bike."
Amonti said, "Honest to God, I never took your bike,"

and he started to cry.
Ali picked Amonti up
and held him close to his chest, carrying Amonti around the ring.
He held him for almost fifteen minutes and
whispered in his ear.
When he put Amonti back on the canvas,
I swear, he floated
and smiled.
Amonti never told anyone what Ali whispered in his ear,
and it's forever his secret …

Years later Amonti was arrested for
Trafficking and Distribution,
and having heroin and cocaine in his possession
and an AK-47 Assault Rifle.
It makes me sad because Amonti is going to do serious
time behind a stone wall and
nobody will believe that he was once held by Ali and told a secret.
Oh, I almost forgot to tell you,
Amonti has a brother who also boxed and could drop a charging
bull with a left hook.
His ring name is "Johnny Good Night"
and he's a preacher and
carries a Bible and in soft whisper spreads the word.

Pure as a Monkey Hitting You with a Hammer

Kitty came down to the gym
because a friend who helps lost souls
and stray alley cats asked me to help her.
She was going to jail for a quick minute and
needed someone to be her soft shoulder.
The bell rang, ending the round,
eight boxers turned and gawked as she stuck out her hand.
"I'm Katherine, but my friends call me Kitty."
I stuck out my fist.
"I'm Dog,
glad to meet you, Kitty."
She pounded my fist back.
I looked at her and
couldn't help noticing she had a fighter's nose
that looks west when the fighter is looking east.
"You used to box?"
She said, "You're staring at my nose.
Nah, I never boxed."
"Well?"
She said, "Oxi-Cottons, I snorted a couple too many."
"A couple?"
She said, "Let's just say I swam with the sharks."
I said, "Katherine is an Irish name.
You Irish?"
"I'm part Irish.
I was named after my Nana and she was from Galway Bay."
I said, "You look Irish.
Your eyes give you away."
She said, "I was in the Irish Smiling Eyes contest,
but I didn't win."
I said, "You should have."
"My Nana wants me to get my nose fixed."
Kitty started to pull her nose east and west,
"I have no cartilage," she said,
with her index finger pushing her nose in,
like she was ringing a doorbell.
"My Nana said if I get off the Oxi's, she'd pay to get it fixed.

I said, "Okay, tell me what happened."
She said, "I got some County time and
got to turn myself in to do some sit-down."
I said, "Alright, you got some sit-down time.
For what?"
She said, "We kinda robbed the lady of her Oxi's."
I said, "Kitty, you kinda my ass.
You robbed the lady.
Let's start again."
She said, "Alright, we robbed her.
'Cept I didn't know he was going to beat her."
"And?"
"I left the door unlocked
and he was just supposed to take her safe and rob her Oxi's.
'Cept she heard him and tried to stop him
and he hit her with the gun."
I asked, "He hit her with the gun?"
Kitty said, "She shouldn't have grabbed him.
He hit her a couple of times."
"A couple of times?"
"He hit her about ten or fifteen times.
I didn't know he was going to hit her."
I said, "He pistol whipped her."
"I was scared and I ran out the door."
I said, "Let me guess:
you met up with him later and got your share of the loot?"
She said, "I didn't take any money,
just got some Oxi's.
I don't even know how much he took."
I asked, "How many Oxi's?"
She said, "About one hundred."
I said, "That's a stack of Franklins."
She said, "About five thousand, but
we snorted a few."
"What do you want me to do, Kitty?"
She said, "Can you ask the judge to give me house arrest?
I got a couple of boys that I put on the bus every day.
And I've been having seizures."
"You have seizures?"

She said, "Yeah, I did some damage to my brain
and sometimes I black out and
I don't remember too much after that,
'Cept when I wake up I have a spoon stuck in my mouth.
So I don't swallow my tongue.
Doctor said I did some damage.
You might say the monkey hit me with a hammer
on top of my head."
I said, "Monkeys do that sometimes."
"Can you help me, Dog?"
"I don't know.
You go to meetings?"
"Sometimes, but I help my Nana and
got to take care of the boys."
I said, "Bullshit your monkey, but don't bullshit me."
She said, "Alright, I hate meetings,
because all the guys want to fuck me."
I said, "That's what guys do."
She said, "I might be an addict, but I ain't no whore."
I said, "Alright, get to some meetings and try to
keep your chastity belt on and
I'll talk to the judge."
She said, "Thanks, Dog."
I asked her, "Did you know the name Katherine means *Pure?*"
She said, "I didn't know that."
I said, "Me either, but
between now and sit-down time try to keep your nose clean."
She walked out of the gym
and I could hear the
tap … tap … tap
of the jump ropes and
thought of a man planting seeds.

Blame It On The Lights

Spacky was training Danny Irish Boy,
at Sammy's Sweat Shop Boxing Gym.
A sixteen-foot ring
three heavy bags
a speed bag
posters of Ali
Marciano and
Golden Gloves.
A sign hung on the front door:
NO SWEARING
NO SPITTING ON THE FLOOR
leather jump ropes hung from a bent nail
a blue spit bucket
and Sam's pit bull Lamatta, who was missing an ear,
lying under the sit-up bench.
Spacky was inside the ring
holding the pads
he was older than laced-up gloves
but could still move like Robinson.
Guessing it had something to do with his tap-tap soft shoe or
maybe from years of running from the cops,
once having been a second-story man.
Anyway,
he was working on a jab ... counter jab
move to the left and drop the right cross
followed by a left hook.
Then the door swings open with a bang.
A fat guy holding a beer yells,
"Whose fuckin' car is parked in front of my garage?"
Spacky said, "It's mine, Comp,
I'll move it in a second."
Fatso says, "You'll move it now."
Spacky says, "When the round's over."
Fatso says, "I said you move it right the fuck now."
Just then the bell rings ending the round.
Spacky steps out of the ring,

"I'm sorry, Comp."
Fatso steps outside the door,
"Listen, you Old Fuck,
can't you read? The sign says,
NO PARKING
and that means **NO PARKING EVER.**"
Spacky says, "I'm sorry, Comp,"
and we know Spacky never apologizes for anything,
let alone twice.
Fatso says, "Move the fuckin' car."
Spacky walks up to Fatso,
hits him with a forearm in the chest
and rifles him with a right hand.
At the same time, Danny Irish Boy, unnoticed, exited the ring,
followed by Lamatta the one-eared pit bull,
all one step behind Spacky.
Fatso then smashes the beer can off Spacky's head,
growling, "You Old Motherfucker."
Spacky staggers backwards,
and before the beer can hits the ground,
Danny Irish Boy, having never taken off the bag gloves,
hits Fatso with a two piece,
and yells, "Good night, Sunshine!"
Fatso falls like a bag of shit,
like he's been shot with an elephant gun.
Spacky starts the Ten Count,
"One
Two
Eight … Nine … Ten … "
Lamatta at the same time biting Fatso's leg
Danny Boy doing an Ali shuffle next to Fatso's head
Fatso's on ding-a-ling tilt his eyes rolled back and
his tongue hanging out his mouth.
Spacky says,
"Hurry, Danny Boy,
let's throw him in the trunk,
I'll get the shovel."
Sammy just then comes walking in,
yells and kicks Lamatta in the ass,

"Stop biting!
Oh! What the fuck did you guys do?
That's my landlord."
Spacky says,
"Your landlord got a glass jaw,
and likes to talk shit."
Sammy starts to shake Fatso,
and starts slapping him across his face,
"Get me some water."
Danny Irish Boy runs and gets the spit bucket,
and pours it over Fatso's head.
Fatso moans, and shakes his tweety bird head.
He tries to get up but falls down again,
"What happened?"
Sammy says,
"The old man hit you but you hit him first."
Fatso looks up at Spacky,
"Old man, you can park wherever you want.
You kick like a fucking mule."
Spacky says, "You should have ducked."
Sammy picks up the blue spit bucket,
"Everybody go home."
Spacky, getting in his car, yells,
"Blame it on the lights!"
beeps his horn and drives away.
Danny Irish Boy pulls up his hooded sweatshirt
and jogs away shadow boxing.
Sammy walks Fatso home.
Everything is gone like yesterday's news,
Sammy's Sweat Shop
Fatso
old boxing posters
blue spit bucket
leather ropes that hung from a bent nail
Lamatta the one-eared pit bull
Danny Irish Boy who made a couple bucks
And Spacky's tap-tap soft shoe.
But we all just know it's the game,
and you never see the punch that floors you

You Almost Bite a Guy's Nose Off

It's not brag or a boast
or believing that I'm the only one
that can see the sunshine in a rainstorm
and can't really tell you why
because I don't know why
I'm telling you the story in the first place …
maybe it's just because I'm supposed to tell you
maybe it's because of Sco
and probably you wouldn't care or
give two hoots
and not give a damn about
sunshine in a rainstorm
… maybe it's only about Sco …
I got a call.
"Yo."
"Is this Dog?"
"Yeah, why?"
"Don't know if you'll remember me,
but you arrested me sixteen years ago."
"I arrested a lot of people."
He said, "My name is Angelo.
I was slinging and running prostitutes."
"Yeah, you had gainful employment,
so let me guess, you want to use me
as a job reference?"
"No, nothing like that,
but do you remember me?"
"Refresh my memory."
"I was fighting with you and
rolling around in the dirt
I had a stun gun
and the girl jumped on your back
and was punching you in the head."
"I do remember, Angelo,
and I'm glad you jarred my memory.

It's a refreshing moment when
I can remember a whore
lumping my head."
Angelo asked, "Do you remember?"
"Of course I remember,
we almost killed you,
because it looked like you were going to shoot me
because you were running with a stun gun,
aiming at me
and I had a punching whore on my back.
Why wouldn't I remember that endearing moment?
It was more fun than a surprise party."
"How's Jumbo and Sco?"
I said, "You have a good memory,
Remembering Jumbo and Sco."
He said, "I remember the fight.
You guys punched me,
maced and choked me."
I said, "You needed choked,
you were running across the parking lot
with a stun gun
which we thought was a real gun
and you were aiming it at me
while the whore jumped on my back,
next thing we were all rolling around in the parking lot,
and you were punching and kicking
and Sco went to spray you with mace,
missed and hit Jumbo in the mouth,
and all three of us were trying to cuff you,
while you were beating us with the handcuffs
and we were all on your back,
you were high on Crystal,
and you were doing push-ups with all three
of us on your back,
and the only way I got you to stop
was I bit your nose.
And putting icing on the cake,
you had a ton of Coke and Crystal in the car."
He said, "I forgot about you biting my nose."

I said, "It was sort of a love bite
and it calmed you down."
He said, "I'm not mad or anything,
I just wanted to call and thank you."
"Not often I get calls from people
thanking me for arresting them and for biting their noses,
it's kind of like a surprise party,
confetti and party horns,
it's kind of an intimate moment."
He said, "No, seriously, I'm not mad,
I called to thank you and take you to lunch."
I said, "You're welcome."
"You guys gave me a break
and I had to do a little sit-down time,
it could have been worse."
I said, "Yeah, it could have been me, and
everybody should get a
second chance to do push-ups with three narcs
on their back.
Whatever happened to the whore?"
He said, "Don't know."
I said, "That's a shame, everybody could use
a good whore now and then,
especially one that can fight."
He asked, "What about Jumbo and Sco?"
I said, "They're both ok,
Sco died on his way to church,
and Jumbo's on a diet."
I said, "He's strutting around in the big whorehouse in the sky
and probably has an eternal hard-on."
He asked, "Are you alright?"
I said, "Once in a while some honey will
drop her pantaloons and
sometimes they even stop over with a
steaming bowl of gruel."
He said, "You don't understand.
I really wanted to thank you,
that's why I called.
You guys gave me a break."

I said, "Thank you twice back."
He asked, "Can I take you and Jumbo to lunch?"
I said, "Give me a call next week, I'll ask Jumbo."
He said, "I turned my life around
and never got in trouble again.
I'm married and have a daughter,
she's twelve going on twenty-one."
I said, "Sons will be sons until they take a wife,
and daughters will be daughters for the rest of your life."
He said, "I'll remember that ... we can go to Eat'n Park."
"Sure, give me a call."
I closed the phone, thinking ... *sometimes you
can get a defining moment,
a surprise party,
and few men get to remember
rolling around a parking lot with a punching whore on their back
and I wonder if anything of this really matters when
you get to walk to the big whorehouse in the sky
just like Sco ... and I wonder if Angelo's daughter
is going to be a cop.
It seems like a fair exchange for a man that ran whores
slings dope and almost kills you
but I'm glad we didn't kill him
or bite off his nose because I imagine
he'd probably be less forgiving.*

Soft Zephyr in Your Pants

It's been said to never volunteer,
but also said that you should always take one for the team.
I also know youth fades away
like a front page news tossed to the wind
and forgotten like an old book in a library collecting dust.
All platitudes like a feel good handshake
or pat on the back,
a quick smile or wink of the eye
and as they say ... when you're gone my friend ... you're gone.
As the story goes ...
the Old Detective sat in front of his boss,
"Yeah, boss, what do you need?"
"I need you to volunteer for an important assignment,
I want you to go back undercover."
Old Detective felt a twang all proud,
"I haven't worked in the shadows for years."
Boss, "I know, but I think you can handle this case."
Old Detective, "Well, I guess,
got to get my old cape and sneakers out of the bottom
of the closet,
and as they say, saddle up."
Boss, "Now that's the right attitude."
"What's the case?"
"I need you to go up to Elk County,
there's an old folks home
called Soft Zephyr Retirement Home."
Old Detective, "Ok, and do what?"
"Well, it's a retirement home for old men
and they're guys from WWII
and Korea and they're mostly there for
Alzheimer's and dementia,
most don't know if they're sipping soup or shitting their pants.
This is their last stop before their
loved ones are planting flowers and cashing in the insurance
policies.
I need you to go up there

and kind of roll around in a wheelchair,
and drool and play the part of a dotard."
Old Detective, "I was thinking you wanted me to be the Night
Stalker, or Serpico, or maybe even something like Popeye Doyle
in the French Connection."
Boss, "No, this is kind of like an old Clint Eastwood,
you know, Dirty Harry, but instead Dusty Harry,
talking to a chair."
"Dusty Harry?"
"Well, yeah, sort of,
I want you to go to Soft Zephyr and there's
an old guy that's walking around blowing all the other old guys.
We got a complaint,
and we need someone with dusty balls,
we know you can do this."
"I have dusty balls?"
"Well, sort of,
you know what I mean,
someone with experience."
"You want me to go up
like Dusty Harry,
roll around and have a guy blow me?"
Boss, "Well, yeah,
but you don't have to get blown,
you have to meet the guy that's blowing all the other old guys,
and maybe just let him put his hand down your pants."
Old Detective, "You want me to go undercover,
play the part of a bag of farts,
to let a pervert
put his hands down my pants?"
Boss, "Yeah."
"I can't let a guy put his hands down my pants."
"Sure you can,
just close your eyes and think of your ex-wife
and it'll be easy."
Old Detective, "Any overtime?"
Boss, "That's up to you,
but you know the rules:
never solve a crime until it's time and a half,

but don't turn it into a Holiday pay."
Old Detective, "Am I allowed to drink?"
Boss, "A little vodka or gin,
but no hard stuff,
and no medical marijuana."
Old Detective, "Alright, but none of the young guys are to know, and the folder's got to be under lock and key."
Boss, "I can't promise that the young guys wouldn't find out, but it will all be lock and key."
"When do I start?"
"Yesterday, and here's a hundred for you to buy
some motion lotion so your balls don't get chapped."
"Thanks, Boss."
Boss, "Thanks, you're a team player,
and I want you to know I'm proud of you,
and I knew that you'd stand up or roll around and
take one for the team."
Old Detective salutes, "For the team, Semper Fi."
Boss salutes back, "You're a better man than me, Gunga Dong."

I Don't Think There's a Law That Says You Can't Shit in Someone's Tuba, But Maybe There Should Be

I found an old police report
about a guy
that wanted to put his brother-in-law through
the living room window.
The brother-in-law
was a tuba player
a portly nerd
and had a fat ass as most tuba players do.
The tuba player's name was Willard.
I asked him, "Willard, why would your brother-in-law
want to put you through the picture window of
your living room?"
He said, "Because he gets drunk
and doesn't like tuba music."
I said, "How do you know he doesn't like tuba music?"
Willard said, "Because he's always
doing things to my tuba."
I asked, "What kind of things?"
Willard said, "He gets drunk
and he shits in my tuba."
I said, "Well, I guess that could be a clue."
"He also hates when
I play
The Lady in Spain
on my tuba.
I asked, "How do you know
he doesn't like when you play
The Lady in Spain?"
"Because when I play
The Lady in Spain
he throws things at me."
I asked, "What kind of things?"
"Things like beer cans,
and one time he threw a pork chop bone

and one time a bowl of Mother Oats,
another time he threw a shoe at me.
He didn't actually throw the shoe at me,
he threw it at my tuba.
And he's always threatening me."
"How does he threaten you?"
"He always says he'e going to
stick my tuba up my ass."
I asked, "Do you know any other
songs besides *The Lady in Spain*?"
Willard said, "Sometimes I play
Roll Out the Barrels
and sometimes I play
Here We Go Steelers, Here We Go,
but it doesn't matter what I play,
he just hates tuba music,
and I'm sure that's why he shits in my tuba."
I said, "Some men don't appreciate music."
Willard said, "I'm afraid of him."
I said, "Alright, Willard, I'm going to lodge
your brother-in-law in the County Jail tonight
and I'm going to suggest that you get
a Protection From Abuse for you and your tuba."
Willard asked, "Do you think that will work?"
I said, "Maybe."
I drove away thinking …
I don't know what drives a man to drink
but maybe listening to tuba music
and nerds with fat asses
that play The Lady in Spain
should be tossed through a living room window.
And then I thought …
I wonder if all people that play
tubas have the same problem? …
and I bet that it would be kind of fun
to shit in someone's tuba
and watch them get tossed through a living room window.
My head started to hurt and I thought,
Maybe I should have been a priest …

Identity Theft and the Vanity of Your Worth

A guy called me with a foreign accent,
I think he could have been from India or
maybe from some country in Africa
that has tigers and hippopotamus'
and he sounded like he was
from a place that I probably couldn't pronounce
wore a seven day shitter
a Godforsaken place where children play in raw sewage
where the men probably stone women for adultery
and my best guess that he had really white teeth ...
because I suspect that most identity thieves
have really white teeth.
"I've stolen your identity."
I said, "You want to be me?
I don't even want to be me!
How'd you get my phone number? It's unlisted."
He said, "Nothing is unlisted,
haven't you read Orwell's book *1984*?
I said, "But that was over twenty years ago,
nobody reads that book anymore, except maybe some professors
that used to be hippies in the 60's
and probably swam in Walden's Pond."
He said, "You only have $22.00 in your checking account,
would you like to borrow some money?"
I said, "No, you can keep the money,
I would only use it to buy tofu,
or maybe a Bukowski or Twain book."
He asked, "You don't care about your identity?"
I said, "Not really,
I've reached the age when I get up to pee
at least three times a night,
and sometimes I stub my toe

which hurts,
but I'm too old to even jump around in pain,
so you can keep my identity."
I hung up the phone,
went to the refrigerator
and found a piece of yesterday's pizza.
I thought of my father … how he'd go to the bakery and
buy yesterday's doughnuts.
It was good except he'd make powdered milk,
which was not really that good,
and I don't even want to mention the government cheese,
but in a strange wino way it was all good.
I lost my balance the other day
and I felt like I'd been drinking,
so I went to the doctor.
I found out it was because my inner ear
had to be cleaned,
which had me feeling almost drunk.
Anyway, the guy calls me back,
"I want to give you back your identity."
"You can keep it," I said.
I hung up the phone
and felt all the pain in my body and
looked up at the ceiling, because that's
where God is usually hiding,
when he's not punishing someone
or curing them from some terminal disease,
and I said, "God, you only punish my vanities.
I should have never danced naked on the bar,
because, truth be told, it wasn't pretty then
and it sure ain't pretty now."
The next day at 5 in the morning
the phone rang.
"Please take back your identity."
I said, "You stole it, you can keep it."
He cried like a sissy who just had his

gym shoes flushed in a toilet,
"But there's nothing in your wallet."
I said, "I told you that."
He said, "But now everyone thinks that I'm you
and I'm getting calls about how a kid was shot
or how a guy beats his wife
or a mother that needs money for her teeth,
another called because her daughter is whoring
and is on heroin,
or needs this or that
and needs help with a ticket for driving the wrong way
on a one-way street.
I now go around sweeping cigarette butts
off streets in Pittsburgh.
I don't even smoke."
I said, "It makes good practice if you can
find the Tao in sweeping up the butts.
It's almost like Zen & the Art of Motorcycle Maintenance,
actually, more like becoming an Archer
or studying the Art of War."
"I don't want your identity,
you've seen stuff that I don't want to see,
besides, your manly
hangs too low,
and when I sit on the toilet it presents a problem."
I said, "Alright, I'll take it back on two conditions.
He said, "Anything, please."
"Promise me you will not vote straight Republican
or Democrat, and when you go to church
you will not stare at women's backsides.
Also, one more thing,
you must read all the teachings of Buddha at least twice."
He said, "Agreed. Thank you, and may the fleas
of a camel never alight on your privates."
I hung up the phone and it rang again,
"Dog, you don't know me

but my son is smoking crack
and stealing Granny's bingo money.
Can you help me?"
I asked, "How did you get my number?"
She said, "I found it in the toilet stall at the bus terminal."
I said, "Alright, you got the right guy.
But try to hurry, I've got to sweep up some cigarette butts.
Go ahead and tell me the sad story anyway,
I need a fix."

Two Thieves

Tommy "Scar Arm", an informant,
would call every so often
when he needed money for a fix
or when he just wanted to stay free and needed me to
say nice things in front of the man with the hammer.
Sometimes he had good information
that could bring down the ceiling of the Sistine Chapel,
but most of the times he only knew who robbed bingo money
from little old ladies.
It was always a crap shoot.
Tommy got his handle Scar Arm
because he had a big purple and green scar on his arm
on account of doctors having to reattach it.
He more or less cut his arm off when he was a boy
robbing a candy store
by punching a plate glass window,
and the glass came down faster than a guillotine.
He was lucky because the little old man
who owned the store stayed upstairs
heard the glass break
and just happened to be a medic on Omaha Beach
and tied a tourniquet, saving Scar Arm's life.
The judge felt sorry for him
and gave him just a lecture
and told him to
stay in school and to go to church,
which was like telling a pig not to roll in mud.
I mean Tommy wanted to listen
and do right
he just couldn't and
I think it was mostly because he was nursed on sour titty milk
and a strap sting across his back swung by a drunkard for a father.
But who can say for sure

Which side of the alley a man should walk?
I guess it all depends on which way the sun shines.
I liked Tommy Scar Arm
and the information that he put in my ear
pinched a couple of thugs in the ass
and made my badge shine brighter
and it did protect those that needed protected.
One time on a Monday I had to attest to his character in
front of Judge Mac
because Scar Arm committed a burglary
and was caught with his hand in the cookie jar.
Now, I know that Judge Mac
doesn't like Cookie Thieves
and he hits them hard with the hammer
and hits them twice as hard on any given Monday,
and they usually are sent away to a place
where there are no cookies.
Well, we were waiting second in line behind
another cookie thief
and Judge Mac started his Monday.
"There's nothing more in this world worse than a cookie thief
and when a man breaks into another man's
castle and takes another man's cookies
there is nothing more low down
despicable
contemptible
cowardly
vile
appalling
and deplorable
and worthless in our society,
like fleas on a dog.
Nothing I despise worse than a common thief.
They are lower than a whale turd
and, if anything, what do you have to say for yourself?"
Well, the first cookie thief in line said,

"Your Honor, I have a problem with drugs
but I'm getting that under control and
I go to meetings and church
and to tell you the truth, I've turned my life around."
Judge Mac then said,
"Well, I'm going to help you go to church
and get your life turned around
5 to 10 down the wall."
Then as the Sheriff was taking him away,
"See that he gets enrolled in a drug program
so he can be with his friends."
Well, me and Scar Arm were next
and I could smell sweat and the fear,
Scar Arm smelled like a bugaboo robbing a grave
on a Hoot Owl November night.
And Scar Arm stood in front of Judge Mac
just shaking and
snot crying and sobbing and tried to speak
but couldn't say nothing more than,
"I'm guilty … *sob* … *sob* … *sob* … Your Honor."
as he wiped away the tears with his sleeve.
I knew I had to say something,
so I said,
"Your Honor, Tommy is a good man
that just did a bad thing,
and he for sure knows how you hate cookie thieves,
and men that invade another man's castle,
how despicable,
worthless as fleas on a dog
and lower than a whale's turd,
and did I say despicable?
He knows sure enough he's despicable
and he's not going to insult your ears
by telling you he's going to turn his life around.
What he's going to tell you when he quits crying
is that if you have mercy on his worthlessness

he will go and work for the man that he took the cookies from
and going to pay him back in tenfold
and never stick his hand in a cookie jar
and will never steal another man's cookies ever again
never again
and will sit on a Bible till his rump calluses
and all his sins pour out from his ears."
Tommy sobbed,
"Tenfold, Your Honor, tenfold, Your Honor,
and the sins will pour from my ears."
Judge Mac looked down at Tommy for more than forever
and it was like waiting for the firing squad to pull the trigger,
"Alright, I'm going to let you work for the man
but instead of tenfold I'm going to make it one hundred,
and if you take one of his cookies
or anyone's cookies you're going to join the other cookie thief.
Now turn your life around and get out of my courtroom."
As we walked down the worn granite steps
Tommy said, "How did you like my sobbing?"
I said, "Pretty good.
You should be nominated for an Oscar."

Basset Hound

It saddens me to get old,
as I looked in the mirror …
and I remembered patrolling the strip mines,
it was all gloom
earth stripped and there were many trees ripped from the earth
and a large blue-blue lake
a bull rope hanging from a dead tree
which I knew to be a danger because it was clearly marked
DANGER
and there were old abandoned cars rusting
rusty washers and dryers
refrigerators abandoned
red steam shovels
hundreds of beer cans
it seemed like the last days of the Earth
desolate like pictures from NASA of an angry blue planet
and my job was to patrol there
so nobody would dump more rusted cars
and kids wouldn't swim in the blue-blue lake …
it was all lonely and days seemed short and dark.
I patrolled almost like a prayer,
half expecting to find Adam and Eve
walking around kicking dust,
lost like having eaten the apple of lust,
or maybe finding an old poet
or prophet or philosopher sitting on a boulder
holding a stick writing something in the dry earth
that would make a difference for all mankind
or maybe finding an ape pounding a femur
jumping up and down like in the movie *2001*,
but it's never that way …
It's just loneliness and maybe a blackbird flying,
nothing more,

or maybe you'll hear the crack of a rifle
but nothing more than the wind of imagination.
It was then I saw a dog
walking towards the blue-blue lake.
It was a Basset Hound.
I pulled up and saw that he was old and dirty,
his ears hung and belly dragged
and he was white mouth thirsty.
I got out of the patrol car,
"How's it going old fellow?
Someone left you out here to die?
You can't drink that water
or you'll die."
I opened the back door,
"Come on, get in the car,
you deserve better than this.
You have a name, dog?
I bet you do —
how about Butch?
Socrates?
Or Cesar or Whitman …
Maybe Howard?
Yeah, let's call you Howard.
That's a good name for you, Howard the hound dog.
You remind me of an old friend, his name was Howard.
He's just like you,
walking around dragging ass.
Howard is a good name for a hound dog.
Man, do you stink!
When's the last time you took a bath?"
I took the Basset home
but on the way I stopped at the store and
got him a dog dish and some cans of Alpo,
and the first thing, "You need a bath, Howard."
Man, did he stink.
I dried him and

got some Brute cologne and sprayed him.
I then got a blue ribbon and tied it to his neck,
"There, now you got some class."
The dog drank right from the bucket
and he gulped the food down like a pig.
I got him a blue blanket
and told him to relax and that I would take him for a walk.
But this ingrate
walked around in a circle
howled like an old French Horn
lifted his leg and took a piss
and then he took a big shit on my new carpet.
I said, "Howard, you are one ungrateful Motherfucker.
I bathe you, feed you,
give you smell good cologne,
and you shit on my rug.
This is how you act?"
I walked to my front door,
opened it and said,
"You and the blue ribbon get the fuck out."
I was tempted to swift kick him in the ass
but he knew, and growled as he walked out the door.
He walked down the sidewalk towards the city
and I yelled, "Bye, you ignorant Motherfucker!
Try not to get run over by a truck!"
Howard never even turned around,
he just walked down the sidewalk like he
owned the city.
Now, years later, standing in front of a mirror,
my cheeks are hung,
big old ears have wild hair,
I'm tired,
and for some strange reason I started to howl.
I let out a deep belly howl and sounded just like
Howard the Basset Hound.

Dog Years and Treats

She's always doing nice things for me,
buys me shirts
and slippers.
Sometimes she rubs my back,
or my feet when they're tired.
Makes me feel like Jesus when the woman rubbed his feet with
expensive oil.
At least I think she does stuff for me,
sometimes she catches me off guard,
and sometimes I can't think straight.
I scratch my head,
or my wrinkly ass.
I came home and there was a candy bar by the door,
and it was wrapped in silver and blue paper.
I thought,
how nice,
what a great gal.
I unwrap the candy,
pick up a book of Bukowski,
and go to my reading room.
I take a big bite,
and start to chew,
it's terrible,
salty chocolate.
I chew harder, and it tastes beefy.
I chew and chew,
and swallow,
take another bite.
Then I chew while I'm reading,
Betting on the Muse.
I put the book down,
read the candy bar label,
Woofer's
There's a dog.

Blue eyes and red tongue.
I read the label,
chocolate with chicken fat,
and dry beef.
Treat for your dog,
rewards for your happy pet.
I call her, "This candy bar you bought me is dog food."
She says, "That's not for you,
it's for Bear."
Bear is the black and white sheep dog next door,
"That mutt always barks at me."
She says,
"Maybe he'll quit barking at you if you quit eating his candy,
and give him a treat."
I tell her, "First of all, Bear is not a him,
Bear is a her.
Secondly, I ate her candy bar."
I hang up the phone,
go to the refrigerator, get out a Coke
and wash down the candy taste.
I read somewhere that Coca-Cola can take up
oil spills in your driveway,
so I guzzle down half the can.
I sat down and continued to read Bukowski,
and his poems about Fante … I wondered if either of them ever ate
dog food …
I put the book down,
go outside and howled at Bear.
She just laid there,
and looked at me as if I were stupid.
I said, "I ate your Woofer's,
So there, now you have something to bark about."
I went inside and fell asleep with the book on my belly,
dreaming of fishing with Chinaski and Bandini,
drinking beer and peeing on a fire hydrant,
and barking at a white moon.

Big Jack

Uptown Gym is gone now,
it was torn down and turned into a parking lot.
It happened after some thug hit Big Jack in the back of the head.
Stole all his bookie money,
left him months in a hospital
and the rest of his life in a wheelchair.
They never caught the louse
and it's probably for the best,
because it only promised vengeance and
false courage to urban legend.
Tar and feathers would have been too kind for the crook,
Vigilantes promised a public lynching,
because it just wasn't right to hurt Big Jack.
I knew Big Jack for years,
I took fighters to the gym,
and I was there when women came to sell their food stamps.
He'd say, "Keep your food stamps,
buy your ugly kids some milk."
Then he'd reach in his pockets
and give the woman twenty dollars,
"You better pay me back,
and try not to hurt yourself when you fall off the barstool."
I was working a fighter
and a junkie came to the gym
trying to sell Jack a big ceiling fan,
"Jack, give me a hundred for this fan."
Jack said, "Go on, get the fuck out of here."
The man said, "Alright, give me fifty."
Jack said, "There's the door."
Junkie insisted, "Jack, give me twenty."
Jack said, "Listen, you dumb motherfucker,
no wonder your mom's always asking me for bail money.
Don't you recognize the pooooolice when you see them?"
I just pretended that I didn't see the hustle,

and the fiend ran out the door carrying the ceiling fan.
Another time, I was taking the fighters away
to the National Championships in Florida,
and was picking them up at the gym.
Darin and Black Joe,
both sixteen years old and full of wide-eyed dreams.
Big Jack asked, "You boys got any money?"
Darin said, "I got fifteen dollars."
Black Joe, all proud, said, "I got twenty-five."
Big Jack said, "How the fuck you clowns going a week to Florida
on empty stomach money?"
He reached in his pocket
and peeled off two crisp one hundred dollar bills.
He said, "Before I give you dummies money
I got to tell you a story.
Black Joe and Darin sat down on two boxing stools,
and Jack asked,
"Do you know what ruins a fighter?"
Both boys shook their empty heads,
and Jack said,
"When I was a boy, about the same age as you two Blockheads,
I met this high yellow girl.
I mean, she was beautiful,
green eyes
and pretty pink soft
long legs fine.
I walked her home
and we both got real happy.
I started to walk home by myself,
and I felt something following me.
I started to walk faster
and I started to get scared
and started to sweat.
I started to run
and could feel something hairy chasing me.
I ran faster,

got real scared,
and my heart was pounding.
I'm six foot eight
and I was stretching my long legs
and ran up the steps.
I unlocked the door,
ran up five steps at a time to my bedroom.
Didn't bother to turn on my light.
As big as I am I got down on one knee
and I was real scared.
I got down on the other knee.
Then I prayed,
'Dear God, take the smell of pussy out of my nose.'
The smell never left,
and that's why I was never any good after that,
and that's exactly what ruins a fighter."
I shook my head,
and both boys started to giggle,
and Big Jack handed the boys the Ben Franklins.
As they were walking out the door he yelled,
"And you better bring me back my change."
He then handed me two more hundred and said,
"Make sure they have a good time."
I said, "Thanks, Jack."
He said, "I was young once long time ago
and I'm just trying to buy my way to heaven."
I said, "I think you just bought yourself a ringside seat."
Sometimes I drive past the parking lot,
and say a little prayer for a good man that lived a good storied life,
who gave much more than he ever took.

Junko the Ditch Digger

They are gone now
street cars
Lemon Blend
WWII soldiers that marched parade on Butler Street
Big Isaly's
Milkman
Junkman
Ragman steel-shoe clomp horsefly drawn wagon
Rags
      Rags
            Rags
Red sky over J&L
hot steel fell over every part of the Steel City magic
Hungarian churches
Polish Holy Family
Irish street fighters
Wiley Avenue Jazz
Jew Town
German North Side Tough
Eat'n Park Girls hopping Allegheny River Boulevard
Forbes Field
Flipping a Dick Groat card
Italian men tossing pennies against the Pleasure Bar
Chucky Bloom Bloom who smoked street cigarette butts
Six Pack Sally with Iron City Beer cans in her hair
Russian John who stood guard at Ft. Wayne
Nummy Clyde who sold papers Downtown,
who spit on himself when teased.
Retardo who would ride the street merry-go-round and scream,
Tokyo Rose who word a short red skirt and held up lampposts.
Roger Tooey who was the meanest-roughest-toughest SOB in Garfield.
Gone like Hey-Diddle-Diddle-Rogel up the middle.
Like Junko from Braddock

who could dig a ditch better than any young stud.
Pushing heavy orange clay over his head at age eighty-two,
hot summer day flannel shirt and grey sweat coal cap,
he'd say in his broken Polish way,
"You need geet strong Reechee.
You need poosh-um-up.
Poosh-um-up Reechee.
Make strong
dig ditch better
get strong woman
and do Poosh-um-up.
Make smile
      Poosh
              Poosh
                       Poosh.
Geet strong like boot suck mud.
You need up-down
Up-down Reechee.
Maybe Polish girl feel good
Dance Polka
Drink beer
Kielbasa
Feel good
Dig gooood ditch."
Red steel sky
Braddock a ghost town beat cop.
And I looked around and Junko was gone,
Old movie houses
and Saturday morning cartoons.

Happy Little Lamb Nursery School

I agreed to come to Happy Little Lamb
Nursery School and read to the little cherubs.
I was to read them
a book I had written, *Drawing in Clouds*.
It was a story of a little boy
who was sad about 9/11
and he was confused about why big people hurt
little people.
How he went out in his yard
and looked at the clouds
and he drew all kinds of happy pictures in the clouds.
How he drew sail boats
and puppies
and fluffy kittens
and how he drew big cookies
and his mommy's hugs
and his pappy's big belly.
I sat with the little happy faces
and told them,
"Nobody is ever allowed to hit or hurt you.
No one is ever allowed to make you feel sad.
You are never to hit or hurt anyone,
and always hands and feet to ourselves."
I told them that they are never allowed to say
bad words
or call anyone names.
Little Amy
blond and blue eyes
raised her hand
and said, "Like the "F" word."
I said, "Yes, exactly.
No bad words."
Then all the other little darlings started to say bad words,
to which I replied,

"Do you know what a zipper is?"
Then motioning across my lips,
"Zip it."
I finished the story
and we sang,
"*I am special do you see*
someone very special
yes,
that's me
yes that's me."
I left Happy Little Lamb Nursery School,
looked at the clouds
and thought …
Let them be little if only for awhile.

God's Gift

I know that I cannot stop the violence.
I know that I cannot stop the violence.
I cannot stop the violence.
I cannot stop the violence.
Stop the violence.
Stop the violence.
I didn't know of Santa shooting the eight-year-old little girl.
I didn't know of Santa shooting the eight-year-old little girl.
It seems so unholy.
It seems so unholy.
I live on the third planet from the sun and it seems so unholy.
I live on the third planet from the sun and it seems so unholy.
It's a grey sky day
cold morning
grey puffs of cold.
December in Pittsburgh is usually cold,
with grey smoke from the chimneys.
It even feels grey,
the smoke feels grey.
Christmas has already gone two days ago,
and soon the New Year will bring promise.
I helped wrap the gift for the earth,
and was told to place it under the tree.
It was a gift from God,
wrapped in gold paper
with a big red ribbon.
You could guess for days upon days,
and never in a million years guess
what's inside the box.
I know what's in it,
mostly because I watched God wrap the gift.
God was thoughtful when He wrapped the gift,
I could tell,
his eyes were sparkling

and He stuck his tongue out of the side of his lip,
as his fingers worked the scissors cutting the paper,
and He folded the corners perfectly
and taped the sides.
He's not really good at wrapping presents,
and He knows He's not very good,
but He asks anyway, "How does it look?"
I, of course, say, "Looks good to me."
Sometimes God has blue eyes,
and He looks up with sea blue eyes,
"Looks good to me, huh?"
I say, "If you already knew the answer, why do you ask?"
He cut the ribbon and took the scissors and twirled the ribbon,
"It's just an extra touch."
Then He sprinkled stardust on the box,
"Perfect."
He said, "Don't tell anyone what's in the box,
let them guess."
I ask, "Can I give them a hint?"
God said, "Only tell them it's the sparkle in a child's eyes when they run with the loud feet of innocence."

A Great Place to Pick Up Chicks is Joann's Fabrics, as Long as You Can Pretend that You Like to Shop for Girdles, and as Long as Your Woman Doesn't Catch You Having Dirty Thoughts, You Could Probably Write a Book

There's nothing worse than
when a woman drags you around
to different places
that you
would never go,
even if someone was holding a revolver in your back,
but for the sake of harmony
you go dragging your feet and pretend that you like it.
It reminds me when I was a boy
and my mother would drag me to Kaufman's
where she would buy a girdle
and I'd have to sit there on a bench
and I remember swinging my feet
kicking the wall
pretending I was sitting on a pirate ship
kicking sharks away
and leaving scuff marks on the wall,
which happens when you leave a little boy
sitting too long while you're buying a girdle.
Anyway, I'm sure all women have this
motherly instinct and
now that I'm a man I can analyze the situation.
Like this woman
who drags me to Joann's Fabrics and
she wants to buy stuff
so she can make things for a party
as she meanders
from sale to sale and
I'm pushing the cart like a dotard

She's almost pulling me by the arm
my legs are heavy
and I'm turning into a zombie
walking like my legs are stilts
and she stopping and picking up everything that glitters
and in my mind I'm groaning
but concealing it well
like I'm hiding secrets from the Gestapo
like a cryptograph film under my tongue
and she turning quickly
I'm sure to catch an expression on my face
and I smile but I feel myself turning into
Elephant Man and I start to swing my one
arm hunchback as I'm bent over
pushing the cart
and she spins and I
say, "I ammmmmmm not a monsterrrrr,
I am a man."
And she says,
"Would you quit it."
and gives me that stare only a woman can make
that's on a mission.
And then God sends a test,
a beautiful blond walks past me
and I look straight ahead
pretending I don't see her long legs
that are connected to all that roundness
and I pretend that I'm looking at a rack of yarn.
And then another fine red head
almost brushes against me
and I look at crocheting needles
then another blond
and a couple of brunettes wearing skin tight everything
and another brick shithouse blond
I start to get hot under the collar
and sin is dancing all around

but I push the cart
in unassuming innocence
like when you walk onto a dance floor
hoping that your zipper is not down.
And then it dawns on me …
that I'm in pig heaven.
All these fillies, and me
the only guy in the stable.
I think what a place to pick up chicks,
this is better than a Family Christian Store,
better than going to a Parents Without Partners Dance.
All I'd have to do is pretend
I like to make stupid shit
and pretend that I'm compassionate to arts and crafts people.
I think that I could even write a book,
How to Pick Up Chicks at Joann's Fabrics
and only spend money on stupid things that are on sale.
I'm thinking if my plan works
I can make money while
getting a woody at the same time.
But all good thinking comes to an end
and it's like my mom
catching me kicking the wall, as
the woman says,
"Stop what you're thinking."
I said, "What?"
And she says, "You know what."
And I swallow the microfilm
and she becomes the Gestapo,
my eyes look down to the floor
and I push the cart
and in my mind I know that I exist in the universe and
it takes a long time for a woman to buy a girdle.

Hospital Gown

I've already told you before:
there's no dignity when you're wearing a hospital gown.
Your ass cheeks are flapping in the wind,
so you might as well just let your pride out on a cold windowsill.
Having been in the hospital for my hip
I can tell you true.
The nurse took me back to the little room
and pulled the curtain back
and told me to take off all my clothes
and get birthday suit nude.
She threw me a hospital gown,
"Put this on."
I asked, "You want the opening in the front or the back?"
She glared with her blue piercing eyes,
"Opening in the back."
I said,
"Are you sure, honey?
I'm hung like a slot machine."
She walked out in a huff.
I put the gown on
and my rump swung free and made me feel like
I was a tuba player
in the Rose Bowl or
just like Icarus being tossed off the cliff by his old man.
An old man, with his ass hanging out
and loss of pride.
Then they took me down the hall on a gurney
to the operating room
and I saw a bevy of babes outside the door
all looking at my butt.
First, I was kind of embarrassed
but then I started to strut, as if you can really strut on a gurney.
But I did turn to my side and pose,
and told a lie.

I told the one young thing,
"You know, I used to be a male stripper,
and danced with the Chippendales."
She looked at me immodestly,
"I bet you were."
Then I asked her, "On a scale of one to ten,
how do you rate the old ham?"
She said without hesitation, "Eight and a half, and
if you were a young stud with a sun tan I'd give you a nine."
A couple of more nurses came in
and looked,
they all said, "Eight to eight and a half."
I flexed the old Gluteus Maximus all proud,
and I said, "If you had a deck of cards
you couldn't slide an Ace of Spades down my crack."
She said, "It would give a new meaning to Texas Hold 'em."
Next thing I remember waking up in recovery,
and as far as I'm concerned, I could have been sitting in a zoo,
whacking off with the monkeys like I was playing
the one arm bandit.
Some things you have no control over,
and you just hope that nobody pushes you off a cliff
like they did Icarus.

Nobody Ever Whacks Off and
Thinks of My Friends

I saw an old friend at the gym
and I ain't going to tell you his name
because it really could be any of my friends
and Lord knows I'd never
ever not ever
want to hurt anyone's feelings,
even if they're dopes.
Anyway, I met this one friend
and I'll tell you this much, he's a half-century old
short runt bent from the years
and he carries a tire around his middle
and he no longer has an ass
his work pants blow in the wind
and he's lost most of his hair
his real hair looks like he has mange
he lost his pride long ago
and most of his women have taken him to court
and sued for half of his pay
and he'll have to work till the day he dies
and with some luck he'll have enough saved for
a decent burial, but probably not.
I asked him, "What's with the scuffling feet
and long face of a horse put out to pasture?"
He said, "I'm down in the dumps because I'm unlucky
at cards and unlucky at love."
I said, "Most everybody I know."
He said, "Can I tell you something?"
I said, "Shoot."
He said, "You know why I'm really in the dumps?"
"Why're you in the dumps?"
He said, "I walked in on my old lady and
she was playing with herself."

I said, "So?"
He said, "She was humping and moaning
she was calling out other guys names
and my name wasn't included."
"So?"
He said, "She was moaning to past lovers."
"So?"
He said, "What makes me sad is that when she finally
sees me I want to join in and she just turned her ass to me.
I asked why she didn't call out my name?
She laughed and said that nobody on this earth
would ever touch themselves and call out my name."
I said, "It's like going to court,
You've got to be careful of the question you ask,
you might not like the answer."
He said, "Then I thought she's probably right,
nobody ever touched themselves and thought of me."
I said, "Not true.
One time you were taller
and had hair
and probably could really put it down.
I'm sure there's a little freak somewhere that
played with the man in the boat and thought of you."
He kinda stood taller, "You think so?"
I said, "Sure, you weren't always a troll."
He puffed, "Thanks."
I said, "Anytime, Dopey, anytime."

Swearing

I like to swear
and swearing should be as natural as breathing
normal as shaking a fist to heaven
Not like saying son of a bitch but more like spitting out
Dusty old balls dragger
Bell's Palsy kisser
Flamingo fornicator
One eye monkey beater
Paper bag full of Shinola
Chrome dome stuck where the sun doesn't shine
Wet pants of a coward
Wart on a witch's ass
Boil on the milk nipple
Turd on a wedding cake
Bunions on the sore feet of a four in the morning streetwalker
Baboon sore blue butt
Bowl of liver and turnips
Pension of the ass wipe of the king
Hung by the nuts from a tall oak tree
Eternal soft-on
Young blue balls stuck to a block of dry ice
Hunchback lover
Club foot up the tight ass of opportunity
Stuttering with a mouth full of monkey poop
Nose picker in school
Booger eater
Snot snort
Bicycle seat licker of a virgin
Taking a steaming dump over a cold bear trap
Sinner locked outside of a church
Defense attorney caught trying to tell the truth
Wet jockstraps in a loser's locker room
Toilet in the bus terminal
Camel toe kisser

Enema bag squeezer
Douchy dude in a pink suit
Double crease shiny silk pants liar
Politician on rusty roller skates
Telling on a nun
Finger up the prostate
Fist up where it doesn't belong
Game of hamster hide and seek
Saggy tits of an old bull …
And soap in my dirty filthy mouth if I don't say
Hot twatty of a tweety scorned.
Now I realize this is nothing like
Stopping in the Woods on a Snowy Evening
or *How Do I Love Thee? Let Me Count the Ways* …
But you've got to realize I've pulled stinkers out of the Ohio River
and cut the rope of the hanged.
Thank you very much.

Condolences Are Condolences

I called Kenny Ken
and told him that the Trooper had died.
Kenny Ken said,
"Man, I feel really sad,
it brings tears to my eyes."
I said, "Mine too, it makes me sad."
He said, "I'm going to send my condolences."
I asked, "You going to send down some money?"
He said, "Hell no,
are you crazy?
I'm going to send down my condolences.
Condolences are condolences
and money is money.
If I send down money
You're gonna have to have condolences for me."
I said, "I understand,
I'll be sure to pray for you."
He said, "Not for me, Dog,
for the Trooper.
Say some prayers for the Trooper."
I said, "Okay, I get it,
prayers are prayers and condolences are condolences.
I've got it now, I'm not to waste prayers,
thinking they're condolences or money."
Kenny Ken said, "Exactly."
"Thanks for setting me straight."
He said, "Anytime, Dog, anytime."

Belladonna on Prozac

An ogre of a woman came into my store,
yet she had a certain glow and a nice smile,
and asked, "Are you hiring?"
I asked, "Do you have a name?"
She said, "Belladonna."
I said, "Have you ever worked in a deli before?"
She said, "No."
I then asked, "Have you ever been in trouble before?"
She said, "Yeah, I just got out of jail,
I'm in the half-way house down the street."
I asked, "For what?"
Belladonna said, "For murder."
"Murder?"
She said, "Yeah, I had to sit for thirteen years.
I murdered my stepfather."
I said, "Well, that's nice.
How did it happen?"
Belladonna said, "He made a play for me,
I was just a young teenage flower,
so I stabbed him."
I said, "You stabbed him."
She said, "Yeah, with a butcher knife,
I stabbed him three times."
I said, "That's nice.
Did he deserve it?"
Belladonna said, "Yes, but the stabbing didn't really kill him,
it was the shotgun blast."
I asked, "Shotgun blast?"
Belladonna said, "Yeah, I jumped on his back,
stuck him three times,
and then on the way down
my mom blasted him with the shotgun."
I said, "Your mom blasted him?"
She said, "Yeah, he needed blasting.

They didn't find the body right away."
Scratching my ass, "Didn't find the body?"
Belladonna said,
"Tough burying the dead,
Yadda ... yaddda .... yaddda."
I said, "That's nice."
She said, "Well, one thing for sure,
none of the customers will intimidate me."
I said, "I bet."
She then asked, "Well, do I get the job?"
I said, "Well, we just hired someone,
but fill out an application and if there's an opening ...
but honesty is important and
you're not allowed to steal and we don't like lying."
She said, "Just because I murdered someone doesn't mean I lie,
or steal."
I said, "That's nice."
I then asked, "How are you doing now?"
She said, "As long as I'm taking my Prozac, I'm fine."
I said, "That's important,
don't miss the magic meds."
She said, "I only made one mistake."
I asked, "What was that?"
Belladonna said, "I didn't bury him deep enough."
I said, "Yadda ... yadda ... yadda."
Somehow I understood.
Told her I'd give her a call if there was an opening,
but we both knew that although there're trustworthy murderers,
and sometimes people need blasting,
a busy deli has no room for lazy gravediggers on Prozac.

Another God Poem

Not another friend dying
or another killing poem
or love poem
or drinking poem
or another lust poem
another war poem.
I want to write about God today.
Maybe like Francis did hundreds of years ago,
how he danced around naked with God laughing inside his heart.
Sometimes I want to be Francis
looking at the sky
talking with birds and wolves.
Sometimes I even want to feel the pain of the stigmata,
and argue with purity of my soul.
But mostly I love just talking with God,
about how He never has enough time to go fishing
or enough time to go to the fights
or baseball game
or go to the horse races.
I tell him I'd buy him a beer,
but He's always busy.
Of course He's always questioned about earthquakes
and floods
and tornadoes
even gets blamed for street violence.
He told me most of his time is taken up drying tears of mothers
that lost their child to madness.
I asked him once if He could stop the tears before they fall,
Turn an upside down frown to a smile.
He told me it's more complicated than that,
It's the grinding gears of the universe
and one day I'd understand.
He did say he does listen to prayer,
real prayer.

Not "I need money" prayers,
but to the prayers of love and pain of distress.
Prayers of worry.
He told me there are many griefs
old age
sickness
hard times
vexation of the spirit
sting of disappointments.
He said that he has an ear for listening,
especially prayers from the heart of innocence.
Sometimes he even sends an angel that will easy the hurt.
He had to run,
but he told me to tell anyone that would listen
He can be found in a glass of water
or in warmth of the sun
or giggle of children.
You've just got to hunt.
I asked him before He left,
"God, can you give me the three digit number today,
I'm not greedy, I'll only bet a buck."
He smiled, "That would be dealing off the bottom."
And I winked looking at the bright edge of the cloud.

Dog is a Love from Hell

Always asking what is the message
asking yourself over and over
What is the message
over and over
again and again
asking and asking
begging for an answer
years turn to years
knowing you have escaped from the fires of hell
and not many would understand
no matter how many times you try to explain
or paint a picture and I'll tell you true
the gates of hell are locked unless you unlock them
having the key
and the key my friend can only be found in your heart
and soul and again and again
the key can only be found in your heart and soul.
To love a God that needs not your love
but to love deeper than the blood of a sin
that kind of blood
that kind of sin.
I guess maybe to understand
you must look into the fire of hell,
and the fires burn deep inside and burn forever
once you have seen hell.
Keep in mind the key …
always the key …
never forget the key …
the key … never forget the key.
Song sung like an Angelus prayer
suffering the incarnation with the pain of oath
and this bell that falls you to your knees
because you have dared to look into the fire.
And always the heat burning deep inside your soul

having touched the scorched earth
and felt the pain of the mother
Mother Earth
and the mother that wailed when you told her that her daughter
had been shot twice in the back of her head
for no other reason than she was just there
wrong place wrong time
and the boy that was shot in the small of his back
and how the bullet ripped through his heart
and how he ran for three city blocks
like a wounded deer
and you followed the trail
and you looked at the blood and the blood had bubbles
and you know that he had been alive for a moment
and fear chasing him
like the echo of the 9mm round that claimed him.
And go back to the drunken negro
that tried to jump off the bridge
and how you grabbed him and held him by his belt
his feet dangling over death
and how you threw him onto the asphalt
and how he brush burned his forehead
dirt and blood mixed.
How you watched as the cops threw him into the wagon
you remember the sound of his body hitting the steel floor
and how they called him,
"You stinky motherfucker,"
and how your heart pounded
and pounded as the wagon drove away
and you sat on the curb
and looked far into the night sky.
And go back to the rockets and mortars
and how you were afraid
praying as everything burned
and smelled of sulfur
and you prayed lying in a ditch

trying to get away from the madness.
Tell of the whiz of bullets
and how you sat on Buddha Hill and watched as the F-100
flew with hundreds and hundreds of bombs
to be dropped from heaven.
Tell them this is the fires of hell
tell them of the Cobras and the red flames from hell
how the flames poured down to the earth.
Tell them of the napalm
and how it burned and scorched the earth.
And the madness has always followed you …
always followed you
like when you found the man in Horne's department store
shaking and stinking
lying there … just lying there breathing like a wounded animal
having shit and pissed his pants.
Tell them of the fifteen-year-old little boy that died
from a drug overdose
and how he had blue eyes and his blond straw hair.
Tell them
tell them of the fires.
Tell them of Jerry
how he crashed on his Harley
and broke every bone in his body
and how you cried, if it matters to anyone.
Tell them of the Old Man and the shotgun trap
and how the man was cut in two
and how his body laid on the dirty wooden porch
with his guts opened to the July sun and how the flies came
and how there was a trickle of blood running from his mouth,
tell them of the fires of hell.
Tell them of the boy that hung himself
in a dirty jail cell in Homestead
and you cut him down
and felt the weight of his cold dead body.
Tell them of Ebony, how she was an honor student

at Westinghouse and she was going to plan her graduation
and she was shot because she was between
the madness of ignorance.
Tell them of Valerie, how she was killed on Christmas
and her last words were,
"I'm hit."
Tell them of George, how he had been shot twice in Vietnam
and once by accident while driving through the Strip District
by some asshole that
was shooting at random and
how the bullet went through his leg.
Tell them how he thought he was being followed by
a motorcycle gang
because he had lost it, his mind was gone and
his madness made him stick a gun in his mouth.
Tell them of Bear, how
he drank himself to death
tell them of Bouncer, how he drank himself to death
tell them of Sabbo, how he drank himself to death
after being held hostage with a shotgun
and how the madman shot the police car windows out.
Tell them about Perry, who also ate his gun on Christmas
but you knew him once when he smiled and loved his wife.
Tell them of Amber,
tell them how she weighed more than the earth
and tell them and tell them
and tell them again.
Tell them of your many bosses that had no backbone
and how they were weak men
so very weak
and they all had high pitched voices like little girls
or like someone was holding their balls with a pair of pliers.
Tell them how you were surrounded and
you didn't belong in the projects
and didn't even have time for a prayer
you had to pretend that you were capable of

blowing their brains out
and you couldn't let a muscle twitch in your face
because they would have seen you were drawstring scared.
Tell them of the body parts found in a dumpster,
and it was a young woman.
Tell them
tell them
tell them.
Go on and on and measure ten times ten times one hundred
a thousand faces
and story after stories you've heard.
Tell them of the oath that you took
but not the oath of man
but the oath that you made to yourself
and how you have felt the stigmata of Francis.
Tell them of the promise that you made,
"No man would ever break you."
Tell them how you have walked the earth inside your soul,
tell them of the promise
tell them …
and again tell them again and again and again that the message
is love
and Dog is a Love from Hell.

About the Author

Jimmy Cvetic worked as an Allegheny County policeman in Pittsburgh, PA for over 30 years, including work as a uniformed officer, a Homicide detective, and an undercover Narcotics officer. He is the founder and Executive Director of the Western Pennsylvania Police Athletic League, and for the past 35 years he has hosted the Summer Poetry Reading Series at Hemingway's bar. During the past four decades he has written over 3000 poems, as well as children's books and plays, while managing a number of boxing gyms throughout the Pittsburgh area, for the WPAL. His multi-media production *Drawing in Clouds,* a 9/11 tribute in 2002, was performed at the Lincoln Memorial in Washington, D.C. A true crime book, *Please Don't Kill Mommy!*, by Fannie Weinstein and Ruth Schumann, is based on a double homicide case solved by Cvetic. His book of poems about Treblinka, *The Evidence Room,* was turned into a play. He is the recipient of many awards, including a Certificate of Appreciation from the City of Los Angeles, a Jefferson Award as Citizen of the Year (an honor founded by Jacqueline Kennedy Onasis), the Kids Need Heroes Award, as well as recognition from the Sons & Daughters of the American Revolution. A Vietnam veteran, Cvetic is also founder of the Three Rivers Peace Project. The subject of a feature-length film, *Secret Society of Dog,* he was also featured in the TV series "White Collar Brawlers". *Dog is a Love from Hell* is his third book of poetry published by Lascaux Editions, along with *Secret Society of Dog* and *Dog Unleashed.*

About the Artist

Rick Bach is a prolific artist who maintains studios in Pittsburgh and Washington, D.C., where he presently resides. *All You Need: Black & White Art of Rick Bach,* a book culled from over 5,000 images, was published by Lascaux Editions in 2016.